D0906037

AARON JUDGE

AARON JUDGE

THE INCREDIBLE STORY OF THE NEW YORK YANKEES' HOME RUN–HITTING PHENOM

DAVID FISCHER

FOREWORD BY BUSTER OLNEY

SPORTS
PUBLISHING

Copyright © 2017 by David Fischer
Foreword © 2017 by Buster Olney

All photos by AP Images, unless otherwise noted.

Sports Publishing books may be purchased in bulk at special discounts for sales promotion, corporate gifts, fund-raising, or educational purposes. Special editions can also be created to specifications. For details, contact the Special Sales Department, Sports Publishing, 307 West 36th Street, 11th Floor, New York, NY 10018 or sportspubbooks@skyhorsepublishing.com.

Sports Publishing® is a registered trademark of Skyhorse Publishing, Inc.®, a Delaware corporation.

Visit our website at www.sportspubbooks.com.

10 9 8 7 6 5 4 3 2 1

Library of Congress Cataloging-in-Publication Data is available on file.

Cover design by Tom Lau
Cover photo credit AP Photos

ISBN: 978-1-68358-236-6
Ebook ISBN: 978-1-68358-237-3

Printed in the United States of America

"Real family does not come from your blood. It is the people standing beside you when no one else is."
—Anonymous

TABLE OF CONTENTS

FOREWORD

JOE TORRE HELD the 2017 Home Run Derby trophy and was ready to hand it over to the winner, and I stood next to him, microphone in hand, prepared to begin the presentation ceremonies for ESPN. But there was problem: the guy who had earned the trophy wouldn't join us.

"Where is Judge?" the producer asked from the production truck, the angst in his voice growing. "Where is Judge?!"

I turned and looked for the slugger, who is hard to miss at 6-foot-7, 282 pounds—the largest position player in Major League Baseball history. He was standing about 30 feet away from me and Joe, his eyes scanning the scrum of people around him. He was also looking for somebody—Danilo Valiente, the Yankees' batting practice pitcher who had thrown to him during the Derby. Aaron Judge would not begin the ceremony until Valiente joined him.

Soon enough, Valiente was at Judge's side, and our TV team could move forward again. Torre handed the trophy over to the slugger. But of all that happened on this evening, from Judge's remarkable splurge of homers to his diminishment of the cavernous ballpark in Miami, his insistence on sharing the stage with a batting practice pitcher virtually unknown outside of the Yankees' clubhouse was Judge's best and most telling moment about who he is.

Judge's impact on the field is apparent to the most casual of fans. He hit more homers in his first season in the American League than any AL rookie ever—even more than Babe Ruth, Hank Greenberg, Joe DiMaggio, Mickey Mantle, or Ted Williams. He scored more runs than any other AL player this year, and smashed the rookie record for walks, which had been held previously by Williams. The day after Judge dominated the Home Run Derby, Reds first baseman Joey Votto—a former MVP generally regarded as the smartest hitter in baseball—spoke with awe as he recounted watching Judge the night before. "I don't think people understand how difficult it is to do what he does," said Votto. "He's amazing."

But the greatest test of Judge could be in how he handles the scrutiny of playing in the world's largest media market, at the center of the most popular sports franchise in the world. When Derek Jeter played for the Yankees, he would receive something in the range of 500 to 1,000 pieces of mail a day, from autograph requests to bar mitzvah invitations to marriage proposals. Judge's natural humility that we witnessed on the field right after the Home Run Derby will serve him well, and even near the end of the first summer of Aaron Judge in Yankee Stadium, he seemed largely unaffected.

ESPN broadcast a game at Yankee Stadium on September 3, the Red Sox against the Yankees, and Judge and his teammates pummeled Boston ace Chris Sale. Judge had been slumping, but in the sixth inning, he clubbed a long home run off reliever Addison Reed. After the game was over and I beckoned for him to do the postgame interview, Judge was clearly surprised; after all, he hadn't been a pivotal performer that night.

"Are you sure you want me, Buster?" Judge said.

"I'm under orders, Aaron," I said, referring to the producers of *SportsCenter*. "They want you."

He nodded and looked down shyly. I told him that we were about 30 seconds from going on air.

He looked at me and smiled broadly, with a purpose. "Do I have anything in my teeth?" he asked, laughing.

Aaron Judge is living life-changing events, and so far, he is unchanged.

—Buster Olney, September 2017

INTRODUCTION

BEFORE THE HOME Run Derby on July 10, 2017, Major League Baseball's commissioner, Rob Manfred, was discussing with a Miami Marlins executive the ground rules for a ball hitting the roof of the retractable stadium atop Miami's Marlins Park. The executive said that no one had ever done it before, and stadium engineers had used NASA calculations to determine a roof height that they felt no baseball could possibly reach. As if on cue, Aaron Judge, who was taking batting practice, smacked a ball off the ceiling. He did it again during the competition, which he won with an awesome display of power. "This is the stuff of Paul Bunyan legend," said Manfred.

Judge's freakish athletic skills were on display throughout his teenage years when he was a three-sport star playing football, basketball, and baseball for Linden High School in central California. The self-deprecating, "aw shucks" demeanor that he exhibits at his locker before and after games was ever present back then too. Judge was every bit the humble and genuine kid growing up. But as one of the tallest kids walking around the halls of his high school, it was hard for Judge not to call attention to himself. He may have stood out at Fresno State, but he did not behave like the BMOC (big man on campus). That is, until he stepped onto an athletic field or court.

As a major leaguer Judge is never cocky or demonstrative. He is a self-effacing, down-to-earth giant, a team-first guy who lets his athletic skills speak for him. Now he is hitting baseballs farther than any Yankee in recent memory, and fans are taking note. They're not necessarily fascinated by the number of home runs he has hit; it is how hard they come off the bat and how far they travel. Judge is the perfect breakout star for today's high-tech, stats-obsessed version of baseball; fans know the exit velocity of every home run, which only adds to his mystique.

This book brings the exciting story of the Yankees' newest superstar to life. The "huggable hulk," as one journalist has called him, offers a newfound sense of hope in baseball and a reason to stay excited through the Fall. Along the way, he has the opportunity to create another storied era of dominance for the New York Yankees.

If the expectations are weighing on Judge, he's not letting on. "The big thing for me this year is having blinders on," he said. "It's tough. There's a lot of noise. But that's the thing, you've got to be mentally strong enough to fight through the noise."

CHAPTER 1

CALIFORNIA KID

A BABY BOY WEIGHING eight pounds eight ounces was born on April 26, 1992, in a hospital in Sacramento, the capital city of California. The next day, Patty and Wayne Judge adopted the infant and named him Aaron James Judge. "It's a miracle," said Wayne, remembering back to the day when he and his wife brought Aaron home for the first time. Aaron was the second child welcomed into the Judge family with loving kindness. Patty and Wayne had already adopted a son, John, who is four years older than Aaron. The brothers grew up in Linden, a rural, agricultural town in the countryside of San Joaquin County, less than 100 miles east of San Francisco.

Linden is a very small town; fewer than 2,000 people reside in the tight-knit, eight-square-mile farming community. Growing up there, everyone knew his or her neighbors. Life in Linden was tranquil—a bucolic place with one stop sign and not a single traffic light. Fruit and nut orchards abound throughout the fields of Linden, where farmers are known for growing delicious walnuts, cherries, and apples. Cherries are especially popular, a prized crop worthy of an annual celebration. The Linden Cherry Festival occurs each May, boasting festivities such as a cherry parade, a cherry bake-off, a cherry pie–eating contest, and dozens of vendors selling cherry-related foods and souvenir items. The fun also includes a 5K run, an antique car show, amusement rides, a parade, and live music by local bands throughout the day.

The town of Linden is a can't-miss destination for cherry-lovers traveling from miles away to attend the exciting annual jubilee. Not long ago, the cherry festival was Linden's biggest claim to fame. That was before Aaron James Judge single-handedly put his hometown on the map.

Growing Up Fast

When Aaron was little, he was big. From the start, he was a chubby infant with a hearty appetite. Late night bottle feedings were a regular event in the Judge household. Aaron's sleep-deprived parents sought to remedy their son's round-the-clock cravings. "It wasn't long before the four ounces of formula was just the appetizer, and it had to be the formula with the oatmeal to pacify him," said Wayne. Soon Aaron was sleeping through the night—and so were his parents.

Aaron was big for his age, and he was growing up fast. At three months, he reached the maximum weight limit for a shoulder-strap baby carrier. At five months, he wore size 12-month clothing. At eight months, he consumed six jars of baby food in a single sitting. He was an easygoing, happy toddler. He was also off the charts in height and weight. At one of his regular checkups the pediatrician told his parents that Aaron would grow to be taller than 6-foot-6. The news didn't shock them. "He was always at the top of the charts for his age group, [with] big hands and feet," said Wayne.

At around nine months, the difficulties of rearing a large child became apparent. People often made tactless remarks like "He's so big!" and asked what his parents were feeding him, as if there was some super food for height. People thought Aaron was closer to two years old than one and wanted to know why he wasn't walking yet. Wayne and Patty politely explained that Aaron was still too young to walk. At three, he was as tall as many six-year-old boys. Because he looked older than his years, adults often expected him to behave more maturely. "He talks funny," they'd say. Sadly, the Judges learned, people can be quick to make judgments based on appearance and blurt out thoughtless comments.

By the time he was five, Aaron was constantly mistaken for a nine– or 10-year-old, not just by other parents, but by other children too. Some were intimidated by Aaron's size, and they shied away from him, especially on the playground. Worries about a confrontation were unfounded. Aaron was a friendly, polite, mild-mannered child, as innocent as a dove. "Aaron has a pretty good compass," said Patty. "At a young age, he knew the difference between right or wrong."

Being so tall was complicated. Kids his age assumed Aaron was older and wouldn't want to play with them, while older kids grew frustrated whenever his behavior matched his age. Some children seemed confused by Aaron's size, unsure of what to make of him. Aaron wasn't so sure, either.

MEDICAL MYSTERY

Patty and Wayne Judge adopted Aaron the day after he was born and brought him back to their home in Linden, California. It wasn't long before they noticed a change happening to their son's body. A large number of symmetrical rings of creased skin folds had developed on Aaron's arms and legs. "We joked that he looked like the Michelin Tire Baby," said Wayne.

Most likely, Aaron was born with a rare pediatric skin condition. The term Michelin Tire Baby Syndrome, named for the cartoon mascot of the Michelin Tire Company, is often used to describe the disease. The skin folds or creases usually disappear naturally as a child grows, which is exactly what happened in Aaron's case. The specific cause of this skin condition is still a mystery. Doctors believe it might have a genetic cause, due to reports of multiple affected members of the same family, but since Aaron is adopted, his family medical history is unknown.

Unwanted Attention

At school, Aaron was always the tallest student in the class. In kindergarten he was the same height as a fifth grader. In class photographs he stood head and shoulders above his schoolmates, and by the time he turned 10, he was already taller than his fourth grade teacher. Tall kids might seem to be on top of the world, but height has its downsides. Aaron couldn't jump on his bed without worrying about breaking it, and he couldn't squeeze into tight spaces during games of hide-and-go-seek. He also outgrew his clothes and needed to shop for a new wardrobe several times a year.

Children come in all shapes and sizes: tall or short, plump or thin. Whether a child is tall or short or somewhere in between, all kids are teased for one reason or another. Kids are commonly teased about physical differences like height, weight, a big nose, having braces, or wearing glasses. And they all want to fit in and be accepted. But when you tower above everyone else, fitting in can be a challenge.

Aaron often heard insensitive remarks from strangers, classmates, and even relatives about his enormous height. Whenever he entered a room or walked down the street, people stared at him. The unwanted attention made him feel uncomfortable. He talked to his parents, who explained that height was just a measurement, and where bigness really counts is on the inside, in terms of kindness, generosity, intelligence, and love.

Throughout his upbringing, Aaron was taught to respect those around him. Those traits are still with the slugger to this day. "My parents gave me the guidance to know how to treat people," he said. "They molded me into the person that I am today."

My parents are amazing. They've taught me so many lessons."

—Aaron Judge

"What's Going on Here?"

As a tall kid in a small town, Aaron stood out. He was different. As a biracial child he stood out for other reasons too. Aaron has not addressed his ethnicity publicly, although he realized at a young age that he did not look like his parents. The first time a classmate asked him why he didn't look like them, he didn't know how to answer. At the age of 10 when he questioned his parents, they confirmed his hunch and explained matter-of-factly that he was adopted. Aaron doesn't recall being fazed by the news. In his mind, Patty was always his mother and Wayne was always his father.

"We really didn't look alike, so I started asking questions, and they told me I was adopted and answered all my questions, and that was that," said Aaron. "I asked questions like, 'I don't look like you, Mom. I don't look like you, Dad. What's going on here?' They told me I was adopted. That was it. I said, 'You're still my mom, the only mom I know. You're still my dad, the only dad I know.'"

Whereas some kids might freak out to learn of their adoption, Aaron accepted the news with grace. "Nothing really changed," he said. "I was fine with it. It really didn't bother me because [they're] the only parents I've ever known. I honestly can't even remember too much, because it wasn't that big of a deal. They just told me I was adopted, and I said, 'Okay, can I go outside and play?'"

As children grow up, they will gradually develop a positive self-image and learn to be comfortable in their own skin. But adoption can present unique challenges for children as they work through the process of forming their identity. Aaron said he someday might seek to help children who are in need. "At one point in my career, I'm going to start a foundation, be a part of something like that," he said.

Some adopted children may struggle with self-esteem compared to their non-adopted peers who have more information about their backgrounds and are more secure in their identities. Identity issues may be further complicated if the child's race or heritage differs from that of the adoptive family. Lucky for Aaron, he had loving and supportive adoptive parents to anchor him.

"I'm blessed," he said. "Some kids grow in their mom's stomach; I grew in my mom's heart. She's always showed me love and compassion ever since I was a little baby. I've never needed to think differently or wonder about anything."

An unbreakable bond has developed since the first time Patty and Wayne Judge held Aaron in their arms, on the second day of his life, when they adopted a second son. "I feel they kind of picked me," said Aaron. "I feel that God was the one that matched us together."

"We're more blessed than he is," said Patty. "Both of our children are adopted. Aaron has an older brother, John, who is teaching English in South Korea, and we're real proud of him, too. Really, it was all meant to be."

Aaron never has had any contact with his biological parents. While some adopted children want to know the identity of their biological parents, according to Aaron, the thought has never crossed his mind. "I can't really relate to it. I have one set of parents, the ones that raised me. That's how it is."

ADOPTION BY THE NUMBERS

Over the years, adoption has become more openly and positively accepted in society. Growing numbers of recent adoptions have been transracial and international, producing families in which parents and children look nothing alike. The attention attracted by these adoptive families has led many Americans to believe that adoption is increasing. Yet the adoption rate has actually been declining.

According to a February 2017 report by the National Council for Adoption, the total number of all adoptions in the United States has fallen, from a count of 133,737 adoptions in 2007 to 110,373 adoptions in 2014. More than half of this decline can be attributed to the significant drop in the number of global adoptions by American parents. In 2014, the number of foreign children adopted by US parents dropped to the lowest level since 1982, according to figures released by the State Department. For comparison's sake, in 2004, foreign adoptions reached an all-time high of 22,884 adoptions. In 2014, the grand total was just 6,441.

CHAPTER 2

SCHOOLBOY STAR

GROWING UP IN the rural community of Linden, California, Aaron Judge used sports as an excuse to stay outdoors. The town of Linden offered its young citizens the chance to participate in many sports—baseball, football, soccer, and basketball, to name a few. Judge played all sports, but baseball was his favorite. The town had lots of open space available for play, and the neighborhood children organized pick-up games for all age groups.

Baseball games were played on one of many ball fields in a public park. Two games were played at once. Older boys played on the big field, and younger children played on the little field. Judge spent much of his free time playing there. It was very clear that he had been blessed with superior hand-eye coordination, extraordinary reflexes, and remarkable athleticism. Hoping to develop his special gift, Judge played baseball as often as he could.

Judge adored playing baseball. He was almost never without a bat and ball. He also watched the game constantly, studying how other players fielded their position and ran the bases. He watched as many games on television as he could. Afterward, he went outside to throw a tennis ball against the garage wall, and he worked hard to copy the moves he saw from the big leaguers. His talent, enthusiasm, and passion for the game soon became apparent. He was a kid who ate, drank, and slept the game. Baseball was everything to him. "I fell in love with baseball at an early age," he said.

Finding Direction

Judge grew up a loyal fan of the San Francisco Giants. His favorite player on the Giants was the shortstop Rich Aurilia, who led the National League in hits and was an All-Star in 2001, when Judge was nine. "My dad's favorite number is 35, so as a kid I wore 35, and Rich Aurilia was the shortstop for my favorite team and he wore 35. I liked watching him." Judge copied the batting stance of his favorite major leaguer. "I was the tallest kid, and I was crouched down like Aurilia. It was funny."

As Judge entered his middle school years, he stood close to six feet tall and weighed 160 pounds. He was often the first player selected when choosing up sides for neighborhood pick-up games. He played baseball, basketball, and football with the older boys in town, and he was better than any of them. His extraordinary combination of athletic power and agility propelled his teams to victory, and his incredible individual accomplishments earned him the respect of other boys. Kids still treated him as a curiosity, asking, "How's the weather up there?" and adults continued to quiz him on his age, but Judge, flashing his gap-toothed smile, took it all in stride.

Judge was a good-natured kid who eventually learned to use his massive size to his advantage, especially when playing friendly indoor pick-up games. When he and his friends played Nerf basketball using a friend's indoor hoop, Judge would dominate the games, lording Godzilla-like over the others trying to get to the eight-foot rim. Another time, a group of boys thought it would be funny to have the smallest boy wrestle the biggest boy. When the match started, Judge lifted up the boy with one hand and dropped him onto the ottoman in the living room, snapping the wheels off the furniture. It was all in fun. Judge knew his own strength and made sure no one ever got hurt.

Because of his size and athletic gifts, Judge was playing sports with boys several years older. He was nine when he played with the 12-year-olds, and 12 when he played with the 16-year-olds. By the spring of 2005, when he was 13 years old, he was a sturdy 175 pounds. He was something special on the baseball field. Judge could run, throw, field, and hit with power. Whenever he'd come to bat, the opposing outfielders moved from their normal position on the big field to near the infield of the little field, nearly 300 feet away. The boys playing on the other field, knowing who was taking his turn at bat, stopped their own games to watch Judge's swings. He often smashed the ball onto the little field.

GIANT MELTDOWN

Aaron Judge was 10 years old when the Giants won the 2002 National League pennant. That team was poised to bring San Francisco its first World Series title before suffering one of the worst meltdowns in postseason history. San Francisco led 5–0 with one out in the bottom of the seventh inning in Game 6. That's when Giants manager Dusty Baker removed starting pitcher Russ Ortiz from the game and made a conspicuous show of handing him the game ball as a keepsake.

By some accounts, that caught the attention of the players in the opposing dugout, and they were not pleased by the exchange. Inflamed, the Los Angeles Angels roared back to score three runs in the bottom of the seventh and eighth innings to escape with a shocking 6–5 victory. The Giants, seven outs away from winning a championship, had blown it. In Game 7, the Angels waltzed past an emotionally deflated Giants team to a 4–1 victory and the World Series title. At the time, Judge was devastated by the heartbreaking loss suffered by his favorite team.

Coming of Age

In Little League, Judge manned first base and pitched. He was by far the biggest kid on the team. Judge's baseball feats began to attract attention. In school, children talked about the number of batters he struck out while pitching. They also marveled at how far he hit a ball out of the yard. Time and again, Judge's pitching success earned notice, and he also continued to impress with his outstanding power hitting. Fielders scattered whenever Judge slugged a ball with all his might. Balls came off his bat so fast there was little time to react. The other kids were afraid of the grass-cutting grounders and screaming line drives he hit, fearing the ball might hit them and cause an injury.

Baseball was making an impact on Judge's life. On the field, he was a success, and he was popular among his teammates. Other boys had once made fun of how tall he stood or had laughed at the size of his shoes—he wears a size 17 shoe! Now those same boys accepted Judge, and his peers admired him. Baseball became an all-consuming obsession for him. The more he played the game, the better he developed his skills.

By the fall of 2008, when he was 16 years old, Judge had grown into a 6-foot-6, 195-pound high school sophomore. His favorite meal was his mom's spaghetti casserole, which he devoured by the tray. Judge did more than play sports in high school. He maintained a solid B-plus average, participated in student government, and was a member of the Every 15 Minutes program, the school's anti–drinking-and-driving initiative. He was friendly, soft-spoken, and humble. He also performed community service. His favorite way to help make the world a better place was to pick up trash with his friends. "That was one of my favorite things to do," he said. "We all got up real early, had breakfast, and walked around the community picking up garbage. We had a lot of fun. It was a good bonding experience."

Beyond his physical attributes, athletic accomplishments, work ethic, and high grade point average, what everyone back in Linden remembers most fondly about Judge is how approachable and sincere a person he was. That's because his parents raised him to be that way. Patty and Wayne Judge worked as physical education teachers in the county school district. In fact, Judge figured he would follow in his parents'—and his older brother's—footsteps as "a science or math teacher."

Education was a priority in the Judge household. Judge and his brother were not allowed to play video games or socialize with friends until they had finished their homework and completed their chores. "They were tough on me," said Judge of his parents. "They'd say, 'Hey, you've got homework to do. You've got to finish your math homework and science homework. Then if you have time left over before dinner, you can go play.'"

For young Judge, it took time before he was old enough to understand the reasoning behind his parents' good intentions. "They helped me try to live to a higher standard," he said. "They wanted me to always make sure I put education first." Now Judge appreciates the important lessons he learned from his parents about time management and the value of accountability. "They made sure I prioritized everything. If I was going to make plans, stick to them," he said. "I didn't like it as a kid, but looking back on it, I really appreciate what they did for me."

Natural Talent

Judge fit in easily with all different groups of students at Linden High School. But it was on the courts and playing fields of Linden where he truly stood out. A three-sport superstar at Linden High, he was the leading scorer on the basketball team, a record-setting touchdown machine on the football team, and the power-hitting first baseman and ace pitcher on the baseball team. He earned state and county honors in all three sports, but assumed a professional career in the National Basketball Association awaited him. "I always thought I'd be a basketball player because I was so tall," he said.

Judge wore jersey number 23 when he made the varsity basketball team as a sophomore, and he proved to be a handful on the court. As the starting center, he was the Raiders' leading scorer, a prodigious shot-blocker, and an unstoppable rebounder. The Raiders utilized his size and leaping ability on inbounds plays, throwing a pass toward the rim so that he could pluck the ball out of the air and dunk it. As a senior, he averaged 18.2 points and 12.8 rebounds a game, good enough to earn a spot on the All-State squad.

Due to his outsize strength and athletic ability, coaches along the way tried to lure Judge in their direction. He attracted attention every time he took the field or walked on the court. Football was not his favorite sport, but as a teenager, it might have been his best. Judge was more than a physical specimen. He was athletic enough that the high school football coach considered making him a quarterback, before deciding his size and speed would be better utilized as a receiver. That turned out to be a good call. Judge went on to break the school records in touchdown receptions and receiving yards.

The Linden football coach, Mike Huber, saw Judge pitching for the baseball team and had visions of a potentially great quarterback. The coach was a friend of Judge's parents, and with their blessing, Judge tried out for the football team as a quarterback. But as many multi-sport athletes discover, the motions for pitching a baseball and throwing a football spiral are completely different. "He didn't stick at quarterback because he couldn't throw the football very well," said the coach. "We made the decision to make him a receiver." Coach Huber allowed Judge to develop for a year on the junior varsity team before calling him up to the varsity team as a junior. He finished that season with 32 catches for 446 yards and four touchdowns. "For as big as he is, he was still lanky and really quick. He could run," said the coach.

"Nobody Could Stop Him"

During his senior year, Judge was a dominant football player. He set single-season school records with 969 receiving yards and 17 touchdown receptions. And he did it all on just 54 catches, averaging a remarkable 17.9 yards per catch. The team's most effective offensive play in the red zone was called Jump Pass. Coach Huber drew up the play to take advantage of Judge's talents. He would line up as a receiver and slip into the end zone, where the quarterback would simply lob a pass, high in the air, and Judge would leap above the helpless defenders and make an easy catch for a touchdown. "It was fun going up against little cornerbacks," he said. "I was 6-foot-7 and they were about 5-foot-8 standing across from me. It was pretty funny."

The coach often signaled the play in from the sidelines with both hands raised in the air. He didn't care that the other team knew it was coming, because they could do nothing to prevent it. "Nobody could stop him," said the coach. Often, Judge didn't even have to jump. By then, he stood 6-foot-7 and weighed 220 pounds. "He was a basketball player," said the coach. "We said, 'This is a rebound for you; just go up and get it.' It was a no-brainer to put him in that situation."

Judge was such a beast on the gridiron that the college football recruiting letters began to arrive in his junior year. Prestigious football programs like Notre Dame, Stanford, UCLA, and Michigan State projected him as a potential All-America caliber tight end. There was always a letter waiting for Judge in the mailbox once he returned home from school. "I got a lot of letters for football," he said. "Every day I'd get letters from colleges wanting to talk to me. It was kind of crazy."

There is little doubt in the minds of anyone who saw him play football that Judge could have had a career in the National Football League, if he had wanted one.

But Judge had other ideas. "I wanted to play baseball," he said. Football was fun, but baseball was his passion.

66

Growing up, baseball was always my first love."

—Aaron Judge

Diamond Gem

It wasn't only football coaches singing Judge's praises. The overtures came from baseball scouts and coaches as well. The Oakland Athletics' scouting department long had been familiar with the slugging first baseman and pitching ace from Linden High School. As a senior, he led the team to a league title and through three rounds of the California Interscholastic Federation playoffs, the best season the school had enjoyed in years.

On the mound, he won nine of 12 decisions with a 0.88 earned run average and struck out 65 batters with a fastball that consistently touched 90 miles per hour on the radar gun and a sharp-breaking curve. Whenever Judge played, it was common to see 20 scouts attending his games. One familiar face was Jermaine Clark, the area scout for the Oakland Athletics. "He was always supportive, a guy who was easy to talk to," said Judge. "I felt like he wanted to get to know me as a person, not just as a player. That really stuck out to me."

Clark immediately recognized Judge's impressive physical tools, and began making plans to closely follow the progress of this high school phenom. There was just one glitch. Linden was a small school and played in a small league against competition that didn't approach the best prep baseball leagues in California. Clark had problems entering information about Judge into the Athletics' database. "I remember putting his schedule in the computer, and none of the schools he was playing registered in our system." Scouts needn't have worried, because it proved nearly impossible to overlook Aaron Judge.

His pitching skills were superb, but it was in the batter's box where he felt most at home. Judge was recognized as a high school All-American in 2010 and was rated as one of the top players in northern California. He posted a .500 batting average with seven home runs and 32 runs batted in. Not surprisingly, opponents often didn't let him take the bat off his shoulders, instead choosing to throw him nothing but curveballs in the dirt. Judge grew frustrated at times, wanting to help his team by swinging the bat, but the Linden baseball coach, Joe Piombo, stressed patience and the importance of not chasing pitches by expanding the strike zone. "That developed him as a hitter," Piombo said.

The frequent non-intentional, intentional walks handed out to Judge were also a source of exasperation for the scouts who attended Linden's games. Sometimes they asked Judge to take extra batting practice after games, because they had seen him swing so little in live competition. The pro scouts insisted he use a wood bat to get an accurate gauge of his power. The Oakland scout Clark was so impressed he recommended Judge to the Athletics' front office. His scouting report on Judge said: "Big kid with a body to dream on. Untapped monster."

When Judge's high school teammates would joke about him becoming a professional baseball player and getting them tickets one day, he would smile sheepishly and try to change the subject. Bragging wasn't his thing. Team success was more important.

THE FIRST DERBY

Judge participated in a Home Run Derby contest for the first time back in high school. At 17, he competed in an impromptu home-run-hitting contest with the baseball team's 20-something assistant coach, an accomplished player in his day. The assistant coach blasted a ball over the left-center field fence that caromed off the side of a building and landed an estimated 375 feet away. The coach walked back to the dugout confident he had won the friendly competition. Then Judge took his turn at bat, and on the very next pitch, he rocketed a ball that sailed on top of the roof of the building! He turned to his coach and with a smile asked, "Is that it, Coach?"

CHAPTER 3
BIG MAN ON CAMPUS

BY HIS LATE teens, Judge had already begun to appreciate his many blessings on and off the field, including his striking appearance. At the high school senior awards ceremony, he went home with all the hardware. The football, basketball, and baseball teams all handed him a trophy as Most Valuable Player. His teammates knew he was college-bound in one sport or another.

There's no doubt that he loved all three sports, but Judge narrowed his choices to baseball and football when the time came to choose a college. He considered Fresno State and two other finalists, San Jose State and Hawaii. There were a handful of smaller schools that offered scholarships for him to play both sports, but he ultimately decided to concentrate on baseball.

Judge's love of baseball from an early age made it clear he was going to choose the sport as a career. His father had told him about former Yankees outfielder Dave Winfield, a 6-foot-6 Hall of Famer who was drafted in all three sports, and pointed to Winfield's comment about choosing baseball because it was easier on his body.

The decision to choose baseball was also partly a big-picture calculation that weighed factors such as length of career, long-term health, and guaranteed contracts—all areas where baseball stands above football as a profession. But those factors, while significant, were secondary. "I had my heart set on baseball," said Judge. "I saw myself as a baseball player. If I had to choose one, it was always going to be baseball."

Turning Heads

For as long as he could remember, Judge has always been larger than life, if not larger than his uniform. Major League Baseball scouts often made the drive to Linden, California, to see the high school supernova. At 17, it was flattering to be recognized by big-league teams. *Baseball America* ranked him among the 80 best prospects in the state. The Oakland Athletics were seriously interested. They had been watching his progress on the diamond for two years and admired his skill set and his makeup. So it was no surprise when Oakland invited the California native to a workout prior to the 2010 draft.

He had been to a few San Francisco Giants games at Candlestick Park as a kid, but he had never been to the Oakland Coliseum before. Excited, he made the 90-minute drive from Linden and went directly to the Coliseum. At the stadium, he bounded out of the dugout and onto a major-league baseball field for the first time in his life. "It was a blur, to be honest," he said. "I was soaking it in, like 'Wow, the grass is perfect, the infield is perfect, the stadium is pretty big.' I was nervous, and my heart was racing."

Judge played center field at Fresno, ran the 60-yard dash in 6.7 seconds, and displayed natural instincts for the game. He also showed the ability to work counts and draw walks and despite a high strikeout rate found a way to hit for average due to a high rate of hard-hit balls. Despite eye-popping potential, Judge wasn't a slam-dunk choice to be taken in the draft. During an age when the majority of top baseball hopefuls grow up as one-sport specialists, playing the game year-round, he was a throwback to the athlete who dabbled in multiple sports. Therefore, his skills on the diamond weren't as polished, and because of his height, his movements weren't always smooth and fluid.

The pre-draft workout at the Oakland Coliseum was an important showcase, and Judge's powerful bat made a lasting impression. Performing on his biggest stage to date, with the entire Oakland scouting department watching his every swing, he rose to the occasion and came through in a big way when it most mattered. "You'd have to be blind to not see the physicality and athleticism," said Oakland's scouting director Eric Kubota. "He's bigger and more athletic than any guy on the field."

Decision Time

The Major League Baseball draft consists of 40 rounds. The 30 teams take turns selecting amateur players from the high school and college ranks. The process takes hours to complete. Round after round, the name Aaron Judge was not called. Finally, in the 31st round, the Oakland Athletics decided to pick the well-built high school outfielder. It was a low-risk selection with unlimited upside potential.

Now the door to professional baseball was open. Imagining a future as a big-league ballplayer, Judge began to fantasize about playing in the Oakland Coliseum, in front of his family and friends, while wearing the white, green, and gold Athletics uniform. Even though he was the 935th overall player to be chosen, it was a huge ego boost to be wanted by a professional baseball team—especially the hometown team.

He was torn between what his heart wanted and what in his head he knew was best. It was his childhood dream to pursue a pro baseball career, and at 18, here was an opportunity to begin to make that dream a reality. But not many players selected in the 31st round are major league ready, and there would be no lucrative contract attached to such a lower-round pick. After deep thought and serious consideration, Judge ultimately opted for college, allowing his parents to steer him to Fresno State University.

"Both of them are teachers, and to them education came first. It was the right decision," he said. "I wasn't ready to face the world yet. I needed to go to college. I needed to mature." It was also important to him that he stay on the West Coast, and the drive to the Fresno campus is only two hours from Linden. "I wanted to stay close to home," he said, "close to family."

Executives in the Oakland Athletics front office knew that signing Judge was a long shot. His parents had already convinced him to accept a scholarship at Fresno State—their alma mater. Jermaine Clark, the Oakland scout, had struck up a relationship with him since high school and hoped he could be convinced to change his mind, but Judge stuck to his plans and did not sign. Naturally, he burned no bridges. "The A's were the first [team] to give me a shot," he said. "I didn't take it, I decided to go to college, but I'll always feel a connection to the Oakland A's."

66

I didn't think I was ready—physically or mentally—to get into pro ball."

—Aaron Judge

THE DRAFT

The Major League Baseball Amateur Draft is held every year in June among the 30 major-league teams. The clubs take turns selecting players in reverse order of their won-loss records from the previous regular season. Major League Baseball's first amateur draft was held in June 1965. With the first pick, the Kansas City Athletics (now Oakland) took Rick Monday, an outfielder from Arizona State University.

Of the four major sports drafts in North America, the MLB draft is the least followed by casual fans. The main reason for this is the draft's overwhelming size—more than 1,200 players were drafted in 2017—and its relative unreliability at projecting a player's development. Players selected in the early rounds are not guaranteed to become stars, while players who are picked in later rounds can. The most notable example of a late-round success is Mike Piazza, a catcher who was drafted in the 62nd round (1,390th overall pick) by the Los Angeles Dodgers in 1988. He finished his 16-year Hall of Fame career with a .308 batting average, 427 home runs, and 1,335 runs batted in.

Leaving Home

Freshman year of college can be a fresh start, something that can present new experiences and challenges to those embarking on one of life's most crucial journeys. But for some young people, beginning the college transition can be difficult. No precise explanation exists for why this happens, though myriad variables are in play, including loneliness and the stress caused by being away from home.

At Fresno State, Judge was in the right place at the right time. After graduating high school at about 220 pounds, he started lifting weights and filled out his substantial frame by adding another 20 pounds. In the fall, he began working out and training with the college baseball team. The camaraderie he shared with teammates helped pave the way for a smooth transition. He and the other Bulldog baseball players often played touch football in the outfield to stay in shape and have fun.

Baseball coach Mike Batesole was in awe of his new recruit's speed and quickness, and he noted that Judge darted past teammates like an NFL running back. Soon the shy player worked up enough courage to cautiously ask the coach if he could try out for the football team. Fresno State had a solid Division I program, and Judge probably could have stepped right in to the starting lineup. But Coach Batesole's answer was firm: we gave you a baseball scholarship, so you're ours.

Batesole was a demanding coach, with a reputation for turning out good ballplayers and solid citizens. He'd coached Fresno State to Western Athletic Conference tournament titles each spring from 2006 to 2009 and won the 2008 College World Series championship. Since taking over the program in 2003, he has produced a pair of high-profile pitchers, Matt Garza and Doug Fister, who toe the rubber in the big leagues today.

Playing college baseball at a high level is a full-time commitment. The competition is fierce and two-way players are a rarity. The Fresno State coaching staff discussed whether the strapping 240-pounder would be more valuable as a pitcher or hitter. It was unlikely he'd succeed as both. For this reason, the Bulldog pitching coach lobbied hard, believing Judge had the size and stuff to star in the majors. Coach Batesole did not disagree, but he was more excited by the freshman's strength and was eager to employ such impressive bat speed in the lineup. The decision was made. Judge became a full-time outfielder.

Difference Maker

Relieved from his mound duties, Judge concentrated on hitting and worked with laser-like focus to improve his swing path. Now he would really come into his own. He played in 55 games as a freshman and finished the season with a .358 batting average and 30 runs batted in, to go along with 11 stolen bases in 12 attempts.

He and his new team were off to a great start. The Bulldogs went 39-14 to finish first in the Western Athletic Conference, and Judge was named to the Freshman All-America and Freshman All-Conference teams. He was also named the conference's freshman of the year. His batting average was the highest among all the Fresno regular players, but he did not produce big power numbers in his first year facing first-rate college pitching. While power was his best asset, he cleared the fence just twice. But he also showed a knack for getting on base and providing solid defense, even when he was not hitting dingers. "My parents always taught me the importance of putting the team first," he said, "but being on those teams at Fresno State really hammered the point home."

Judge shouldered great expectations for the 2012 season. *College Baseball Insider* named him a preseason honorable mention All-American. In a move he hoped would help improve his power numbers even more, he continued to hit the weight room and pack on the muscle. He did not look like a player only two years removed from high school. The college sophomore stood a whopping 6-foot-7 and weighed in at 255 pounds, a 15-pound increase from the year before.

Now 20, he began to finally make strides as a power hitter. The coach inserted him into the No. 3 position in the batting order, a major shift from the No. 7 slot he held as a freshman. With the added responsibility, his average dipped to .308 but he had 20 extra-base hits, including four home runs. He slugged two homers in one game against Stanford's Mark Appel, the first pick in the nation in the 2013 draft. He also drew a team-high 48 walks and stole 13 bases in 15 attempts.

His massive size and strength stood out, but so too did his baserunning acumen. In college, he had an 88 percent success rate stealing bases. He stole twice as many bases (36) as he hit home runs (18) while wearing a Bulldogs uniform.

The Fresno State Bulldogs captured the conference championship crown for a second year in a row and reached the regional round at the College Baseball World Series. Leading the way was number 29, Aaron Judge, named to the All-Conference tournament team and to the All-Conference team for a second straight season. Later that summer he joined the Brewster Whitecaps of the Cape Cod League, a veritable training ground for potential draftees. More than 250 Cape League alumni are active players on major-league rosters.

BASEBALL AT THE BEACH

The Cape Cod League is one of 11 summer leagues sanctioned by the National Collegiate Athletic Association. While other leagues have been summer homes to future big leaguers, none have more former players in the majors than the Cape League. In all, more than 1,100 Cape League alums have gone on to play in the major leagues.

In 2015, 14 Cape League alumni were selected to the Major League Baseball All-Star Game in Cincinnati, including four starters: National League third baseman Todd Frazier (Chatham, 2005–2006), NL catcher Buster Posey (Yarmouth-Dennis, 2006–2007), American League third baseman Josh Donaldson (Harwich, 2006), and AL pitcher Dallas Keuchel (Wareham, 2007–2008).

Cooperstown inductees have played on the Cape (Craig Biggio, Carlton Fisk, Frank Thomas, and Jeff Bagwell), along with retired All-Stars (Albert Belle, Lance Berkman, Will Clark, Nomar Garciaparra, and Jason Varitek) and Cy Young Award winners (Barry Zito and Tim Lincecum).

The Big Bopper

Cape Cod is a peninsula on the southeastern corner of Massachusetts and a popular summer beach destination. Tourists come in waves to frolic in the surf while amateur ballplayers compete like sharks to gain the notice of pro baseball scouts. On the Cape, Judge came in like a crashing wave. He posted a .270 batting average in 32 Cape League games, with five home runs and 16 runs batted in. He was named the team's Citizenship Award winner for being a good teammate. *Baseball America* ranked him the sixth-best prospect in the league.

"Judge's combination of size (6-foot-7, 255 pounds) and athleticism is so unusual for a baseball player that the comparison scouts make most is to NBA star Blake Griffin," read the article. "With his leverage and strength, Judge can hit tape-measure shots most players only can dream of."

Judge's size and strength stood out, but it was also good sportsmanship, smart baseball instincts, and being a supportive teammate that led many observers to see him as a special talent. Judge's years at Fresno State introduced him to the kangaroo court, where teammates were fined for infractions of baseball etiquette. Players had to put a dollar in a shoebox every time they were punished for missing a sign or throwing to the wrong base. Everyone slipped up at least a few times a season. In three years as a Bulldog, Judge was never fined.

While at Cape Cod, he was among a small group of players invited to take batting practice at Fenway Park in Boston one day when the Red Sox were away. The display of power was not soon forgotten. He deposited ball after ball deep in the seats and against and over the Green Monster in left field. "He was rattling balls up in the lights," said Damon Oppenheimer, scouting director for the New York Yankees. "His tools were all there."

With that size comes sheer strength, and with strength, Judge can hit the ball harder than most anyone. That not only means more home runs, but with the ball coming off the bat faster, it increases the chances of batted balls being hit out of the fielders' reach. If spectators weren't already gazing in wonder at Judge, they would be after seeing him smash several balls into the stratosphere during the College Baseball Home Run Derby. He was one of eight players selected to participate in the event in Omaha, Nebraska, on July 3, 2012. That night in Omaha remains a cherished memory for Judge.

Down to his last out and trailing by one home run, Judge hit four consecutive balls out of the ballpark, much to the delight of the 22,403 fans in attendance. It was by far the biggest crowd for which Judge had performed. "In college, on good nights, maybe you'd have 10,000 people," he said. "After you hit one and two and three, they get a little excited and you can hear them, and you feed off that."

Judge won the event by blasting a total of 16 home runs in the three-round competition. The result was no surprise to Louisiana State's Mason Katz and Virginia Tech's Tyler Horan, the two players he beat out in the three-player final round. "Judge makes it look so easy," said Katz. Prior to the event, he introduced himself to Judge. "He stood up to shake my hand, and I remember looking straight up," said Katz, who is 5-foot-9. "I was like, 'This is gonna be a fun derby.'" Afterward, when Horan congratulated Judge and shook his hand, he said, "It felt like I was shaking an outfielder's mitt instead of somebody's hand."

As Judge posed with the trophy after winning the 2012 College Baseball Home Run Derby, colorful fireworks exploded high above the stadium. The 20-year-old has always had a flair for the dramatic, and his eye-popping derby display firmly put him back on the radar of professional scouts. The Major League Baseball draft was on the horizon, and for Judge the sky was the limit.

CHAPTER 4

PLAYING FOR A LIVING

JUDGE TURNED MANY heads with his power stroke, and he helped lead the Fresno State Bulldogs to appearances in the 2011 and 2012 College World Series. He reached new heights in 2013, mashing 12 home runs and pacing the Bulldogs in hits, doubles, home runs, runs batted in, runs scored, slugging percentage, walks, and stolen bases. He batted .369, also a team high, but it was an on-base percentage of .461 that really stood out. "That's what wins ballgames," he said. "If you get on base, the guys behind you can drive you in."

The awards and accolades continued rolling in for the 21-year-old slugger. Fresno State now played in the Mountain West Conference, and it was a no-brainer when the junior outfielder was selected as a first-team All-Conference player for a third consecutive season. His abilities and body matured in college, which led major-league scouts to project unlimited upside potential once he fully developed and made the adjustments necessary for a successful career in pro ball.

"The decision to go to school worked out in a lot of ways," said Judge, who finished his collegiate career with a .345 batting average, 18 home runs, and 93 runs batted in. "I definitely became a leader during those years. I was fully ready to play professional baseball."

When he arrived in New York City to attend the 2013 draft, it was a time of anticipation and uncertainty. Experts predicted he would be picked in the first round of the draft, but by which team was anybody's guess. As a kid from a small town where everyone knows everyone else, it was understandable that he felt a bit overwhelmed in the big city with so many people, cars, and tall buildings surrounding him. "It's too busy, seems hectic," he said. "I'm not sure I could ever live here."

Risky Move

The New York Yankees zeroed in on Judge and selected him with the 32nd overall pick of the draft, meaning that 31 times an MLB team decided to take someone else. He was the second player the Yankees took in the draft, after selecting Notre Dame third baseman Eric Jagielo with the 26th pick. The Yankees then held their breath that Judge would be there for them six picks later. That was a risky move and no sure thing.

The Yankees sweated out the next five picks and then, with a sigh of relief, called out Judge's name. New York nabbed their man. Judge signed a professional baseball contract and got a $1.8 million signing bonus. It was the sixth-highest signing bonus the Yankees had ever given a drafted player. Visions of a 6-foot-7 behemoth wearing pin-stripes and one day swinging for the fences in the Bronx was an exhila-rating thought. "Raw power like that is so hard to find," said Damon Oppenheimer, the Yankees scouting director. Now there are 29 other teams kicking themselves for missing out on a future superstar.

Three years after being drafted by the Oakland Athletics, Judge was in New York Yankees gear and taking batting practice at the Oakland Coliseum. It was three days after the draft, and coincidentally, the Yankees were in Oakland to play a series against the Athletics. Judge and his parents made the short drive to the Coliseum where he got his first taste of the big-league atmosphere. "Words really can't describe that feeling, being out there with all the big guys," he said. "Being on a major-league field, putting on a jersey, and having my own name up on a locker next to Mariano [Rivera] and Andy Pettitte. That was an unreal moment. I was speechless." Judge took batting practice with the big club in front of Yankees manager Joe Girardi. It was the highlight of his professional career to that point.

Lucky Break

The Yankees assigned Judge to the Charleston RiverDogs, their minor-league affiliate in Charleston, South Carolina. The team plays in the Single-A South Atlantic League, the lowest rung on the pro baseball ladder. Before he could take the field in 2013, he tore his right quadriceps muscle and was shut down for the rest of the season. He was unlikely to get healthy in time to appear in any minor-league games, so the club simply decided not to push it. That turned out to be a blessing in disguise. While rehabbing the leg injury at the team's minor-league facility, in Tampa, Florida, he found himself reporting to the same training room as star shortstop Derek Jeter, who was recovering from his own injury, a fractured ankle suffered in the 2012 postseason.

Judge took advantage of the time he spent with Jeter, picking his brain for tips on what it takes to get to the majors. "He and I talked about what he had done to be successful year in and year out," he said. "I know it's going to help me down the road." Some of the best advice Jeter gave the young prospect was to have a short memory. "He told me to keep an even keel, don't get too high or too low," he said. "Forget about what happened the day before. Everyone is going to have ups and downs. You keep grinding it out, stay consistent, that's the key to a long career."

66

Words can't describe how valuable that time was with [Jeter]."

—Aaron Judge

The injury shortly after signing his contract delayed Judge's debut in pro ball until spring 2014. Among his teammates at Charleston was pitching prospect Luis Severino, who had already been in the minors for two years. Showing no ill effects from the setback, Judge proved he was ready to rock. In 65 games, he batted .333 with nine home runs and 45 runs batted in. Those consistent numbers and a balanced approach at the plate soon earned him a midseason promotion to the High-A Tampa Yankees, where he joined power-hitting first baseman Greg Bird on a club managed by Al Pedrique. The move didn't slow him down, as he batted .283 and cleared the fence eight times, more than holding his own against better pitching in the Florida State League.

The hitting coach for the Tampa Yankees, P. J. Pilittere, learned right away what type of teammate Judge was. "In his first game, he came up in a big spot, and he didn't get the job done," said the coach. "He came back to the dugout, put his helmet and bat away and immediately started cheering for the next guy at the plate. That told me all I needed to know about him." Coach Pilittere played eight seasons in the Yankees' minor-league system, attending big-league camp with the likes of Jeter and Jorge Posada. He believed Judge's temperament was ideal. "The good ones that play this game can control their emotions; it's a special talent. The fact that he can already do it is a promising sign of things to come."

CHART TOPPER

During home games a baseball player will approach home plate with a song that he selected playing over the stadium's speaker system. A player's "walk-up song" can be an indication of his personality.

During the spring of 2014, whenever Aaron Judge took his turn at bat, the loudspeaker at Joseph P. Riley Jr. Park, in Charleston, South Carolina, blared "Timber," a song by rapper Pitbull featuring Kesha. "Timber" held the number one spot on the Billboard 100 chart for three weeks earlier in the year.

With its lyrics about cutting down a tree, the song was a perfect fit for the rookie with the Paul Bunyan physique.

Bright Future

The first year of pro ball was a learning experience for which Judge received high marks. He made two stops, in Charleston and Tampa, and finished the 2014 season with a .308 batting average, 17 home runs, and 78 runs batted in. *Baseball America* now rated him the sixth-best Yankees prospect. His combination of mammoth size and super-human strength, along with his quick hands, made him one of the premier power hitters in the Yankees farm system. His batting practice sessions before games and during practices became must-see viewing for not only his teammates, but opposing teams as well. "When he gets ahold of a ball, he can hit it a mile," said a Charleston teammate.

Judge was already being compared to Miami Marlins slugger Giancarlo Stanton, who is an inch shorter but 35 pounds lighter than Judge. In the 2014 season with the Marlins, Stanton smashed a National League–leading 37 homers and finished second in the Most Valuable Player balloting. "I can see similarities between Giancarlo and

Aaron," said RiverDogs manager Luis Dorante, who was working in the Marlins organization when Stanton was coming up through their farm system. "They are about the same size and both have tremendous power and very good hands. I think Aaron has that kind of potential."

Yet for all his prodigious power, the 22-year-old right-handed batter still was figuring it out. He was selective and drew his share of walks, but he also let too many hittable pitches go by, and quality inside fastballs often tied him up. Few doubted that Judge had a bright future with the Yankees organization, though he remained very much a work in progress. "At first, the biggest adjustment from college was the number of games that are played in pro ball," he said. "Going from three or four games a week to playing every day took some getting used to. But once I began to focus, I got into a good routine."

His powerful bat left a lasting impression on the Yankees during spring training in March 2015. In big-league camp for the first time, he did all he could to take advantage of the opportunity. In the preseason opener against the Philadelphia Phillies, he entered the game in the sixth inning as a pinch-hitter. "My emotions were all over the place when I came to the plate," he said. "But once I saw a few pitches, I said to myself, 'This is the same game you've always played your whole life.' Then I was able to calm down." With New York losing by three runs and down to its last out in the ninth inning, he hit a towering three-run blast into the left-center field bullpen to tie the game. Patty and Wayne Judge were there to share in the celebration. "It's been off-the-charts fun seeing Aaron play," said Patty.

After tearing the cover off the ball in spring training, his stock rocketed. At every level Judge not only hit tape-measure home runs, but he also proved himself to be an excellent outfielder with an accurate throwing arm. Better still, practically everyone who came in contact with him raved about his "makeup": the combination of intellect, humility, and drive that allowed for a meteoric rise within the team hierarchy.

Even so, with patience a virtue, Judge knew he would be assigned to the Trenton Thunder, the Yankees Double-A team, when spring training camp broke. The Yankees were top-heavy with aging veterans, creating a logjam in the big-league outfield. But Judge was dreaming big and willing to put in the work to achieve it. "This is where we all want to be," he said of his first Yankees camp. "Getting a taste of it here, I want more. Now I have to go out there and get it."

Rising Star

Even though he was now rated by *Baseball America* as the club's top position prospect, the Yankees ticketed Judge to New Jersey to play in the Eastern League. Once there, he continued to make a lasting impression. He marked his first game in a Trenton uniform by corking a three-run bomb, and a few days later, he hit a walkoff blast in the team's home opener. Judge recorded a 14-game hitting streak with the Thunder in the first half of May, going 21-for-58 over that span (.362). Overall, the 23-year-old batted .284 with 44 runs batted in and walloped 12 home runs in 63 games. He was slugging over .500 and leading the Eastern League in home runs when he was promoted to the Triple-A Scranton/Wilkes-Barre RailRiders, where he was reunited with first baseman Greg Bird.

The shadow cast by his rapid rise grew yet again when, a few weeks after the promotion, he and catcher Gary Sanchez were chosen to represent the Yankees at the 2015 Futures Game, which was to be played at Great American Ballpark, in Cincinnati, Ohio, on the Sunday before the major-league All-Star Game. The Futures Game pits the best minor-league prospects from the United States against a team of prospects from other countries. Judge was humbled and excited by the honor.

"I called my parents and said, 'I don't know what the weather is going to be like in Cincinnati, but you need to pack your bags.'" Their son collected one single in four at-bats in the game and was grateful for the opportunity. "You always want to play against the best," he said.

Possessing the work ethic of a small-town kid was starting to pay dividends.

According to MLB.com, he was now rated among the top 60 prospects in all of Major League Baseball, solidifying him as a rising star in an organization desperate for one. The Yankees hadn't drafted and developed an All-Star player since the famed "Core Four" of Jeter, Pettitte, Rivera, and Posada. That foursome forged the backbone of the Yankees' late-1990s dynasty that won four World Series championships in five years.

Now the "Core Four" was gone, having long since retired, leaving fans to wonder if Judge would be the next homegrown star. "That's everybody's dream," he said. "Even as a little kid, you want to grow up and be one of the legends, one of the greatest of all time. One of my dreams is to be one of the next great ones, but I know I have to work hard every day to work toward that goal."

THE CORE FOUR

At a time when the New York Yankees had not played in a World Series in 14 years—the Bronx Bombers' longest drought since before the days of Babe Ruth—along came four young players whose powerful impact returned the franchise to its former glory. They were a diverse group from different parts of the globe: Mariano Rivera, a right-handed pitcher from Panama, who was destined to become baseball's all-time saves leader; Derek Jeter, a shortstop raised in Kalamazoo, Michigan, who would become the first Yankee to accumulate 3,000 hits; Jorge Posada, an infielder-turned-catcher from Puerto Rico, who would hit more home runs than any Yankees catcher except the legendary Hall of Famer Yogi

Berra; and Andy Pettitte, a left-handed pitcher born in Baton Rouge, Louisiana, who would win more postseason games than any pitcher in baseball history. Together they formed the "Core Four," playing as teammates for 13 seasons, helping the Yankees advance to the postseason 12 times, winning the American League pennant seven times, and taking home five World Series trophies.

CHAPTER 5
THE YANKEES CALL

JUDGE STEADILY MOVED through the New York Yankees minor-league system and helped the Scranton/Wilkes-Barre RailRiders capture the International League's North Division flag. Splitting time between Double-A and Triple-A, he finished the 2015 season with a combined .255 batting average, 20 home runs, and 72 runs batted in. His fierce drive to succeed was as important to his progress as his raw talent. "I come to the park every day with the goal of being better than I was the day before," he said. "I feel that if I can do that each day, I will get to where I want to be."

Reaching the level one step away from the major leagues in just his second season of professional baseball was a thrill, but Judge stalled a bit during his first stint with the RailRiders. His power numbers were there—he blasted eight home runs in 61 games—but his batting average sank to a mere .224, and he struck out an alarming 74 times. Strikeouts were a big problem. His size might have been part of the issue. At 6-foot-7, he presented a huge strike zone, which was exploited by the shrewder Triple-A pitchers. He also showed a troubling tendency to chase pitches out of the strike zone. Despite an unexpected slowdown to his rapid ascent, the Yankees' highly touted prospect never lost confidence. "Time will tell," said Judge. "I try not to think about playing in the majors. I try to focus on being where my feet are. That's what's gotten me this far."

Minor Adjustments

Leaning on his reputation as one of baseball's best prospects, climbing from Single-A to Triple-A in just over a year, Judge never wavered from his one-day-at-a-time approach to the game. After scuffling at Scranton/Wilkes-Barre in the second half of 2015, he worked diligently on his mechanics and approach all winter to adjust to the more advanced pitching he was facing, and he came back as one of the league's premier power hitters. In particular, he made great strides in improving his plate discipline. Now he swung at more strikes, took more balls, and better recognized breaking pitches, which allowed him to post a higher batting average and better power numbers, since he was swinging at better pitches to hit.

66

I come to the park every day with the goal of being better than I was the day before."

—Aaron Judge

The fine-tuning paid immediate dividends in 2016. Judge was the International League's top home-run hitter when he was named to the Triple-A All-Star team. The 24-year-old mega prospect got hurt diving for a ball near the warning track and did not participate in the game due to a mild sprain and bone bruise of the right knee. He returned to the lineup one week later without missing a beat. In 93 games with the RailRiders, he boasted a .270 batting average, 19 home runs, and 65 runs batted in. Following the season he was named the International League's "Best Power Prospect." Judge had now hit 56 home runs over three minor-league seasons, and he thought a trip to the Bronx might not be so far off.

Meanwhile, back in the Bronx, the 2016 season was a transition year for the New York Yankees. The lineup had become a collection of decorated but aging sluggers. Prior to the July trade deadline, general manager Brian Cashman decided the Yankees would be sellers for the first time in over 25 years and committed fully to a youth movement that figured to pan out over the next few years. Pitchers Aroldis Chapman, Andrew Miller, and Ivan Nova and outfielder Carlos Beltran were all traded to other contending teams in return for highly touted prospects. As part of their sudden youth movement, the Yankees also released third baseman Alex Rodriguez, who had 696 career home runs—trailing only Babe Ruth (714), Hank Aaron (755), and Barry Bonds (762) on the all-time list. The team called up catcher Gary Sanchez on August 3 and 10 days later plucked two more players off their Triple-A roster.

The Scranton/Wilkes-Barre RailRiders had beaten the Rochester Red Wings, 12–7, on a Friday night in Rochester, New York, on August 12, 2016. After the game, Judge, who had homered and scored four runs, was sharing a late-night meal with his parents when his cell phone rang with the news he had worked and hoped for his entire life. Calling was manager Al Pedrique to inform him he was expected in the Bronx the following day. "When I got told, it was pretty crazy," he said. The Judges drove from Rochester five hours south to Yankee Stadium for a Saturday day game against the Tampa Bay Rays. The Yankees also brought up first baseman Tyler Austin the same day.

When Judge arrived, the atmosphere was electric—not because a 6-foot-7 giant had just entered the Yankees clubhouse, but because of the presence of members of the 1996 World Series winning team, who were being honored before the game. The ceremony might have been billed as a celebration of the past, commemorating 20 years since that 1996 squad had ushered in another era of dominance. Instead, all of those Yankees greats were about to get a glimpse of the future.

NUMBER 99

Aaron Judge wears number 99, but the number was not his personal choice. Rather, it was the rookie number that was handed to him during spring training in 2016. "They gave it to me in spring training and it just kind of stuck with me," he said. Judge also wore number 99 as a member of the Scranton/Wilkes-Barre Yankees in Triple-A.

Judge is just the 17th player in the history of Major League Baseball to wear the number. Former reliever Brian Bruney was the last Yankee to wear number 99 before Judge, in 2009. Charlie Keller also wore number 99 in 1952 and was the first player in MLB history to wear it.

Judge previously said he would prefer to wear either number 44 or number 35. While Judge's Twitter handle, @TheJudge44, shows off his fondness for that number, "My favorite always has been 35," he said. Both were unavailable—number 44 was retired by the Yankees in 1993 to honor Reggie Jackson and number 35 has been worn by pitcher Michael Pineda since 2014. Pineda can become a free agent after the 2017 season, but Judge may not be keen on switching anymore. He recently said number 99 has grown on him.

Stunning Start

On the same day the Yankees honored their 1996 World Series championship team, a new era of Yankees baseball began with a bang. Tyler Austin and Judge did not wait long to prove they belonged in the major leagues, making their debuts in stunning fashion during the Yankees' 8–4 win at Yankee Stadium, on August 13, 2016.

The teammates hammered back-to-back home runs in their first at-bats in the second inning to give New York a 2–0 lead. Austin and Judge became the first teammates to hit home runs in their first major-league at-bats in the same game. Judge was so stunned he nearly tripped over second on his way around the bases. They also were the first teammates to homer in their debuts in the same game and became the fourth and fifth players in Yankees history to hit home runs in their first career plate appearance, joining John Miller, Andy Phillips, and Marcus Thames.

"You can't draw it up any better when you call up two young players," said Yankees manager Joe Girardi.

With two outs in the second inning, Austin faced Rays right-hander Matt Andriese and with a 2-2 count drove a 92-mile-per-hour fastball just over the 314-foot sign near the foul pole in right field, which prompted Austin to pump his fist in celebration. "I don't think I could've asked for anything better," Austin said. "It's pretty awesome."

Then Judge stepped into the batter's box for the first time as a major leaguer in Yankee Stadium. He was excited and nervous. The fans were still buzzing about Austin's historic homer. With a 1-2 count, Andriese tried to fool Judge with an off-speed pitch, but Judge waited on the pitch and caught it square. He connected with Andriese's 87-mile-per-hour changeup and drilled a breathtaking blast that traveled 457 feet over the center field wall. "It was exciting," he said. "Tyler went out there and he got down 0-2 really quick, but he battled and had a great at-bat and was able to hit one out. I was ecstatic on deck and I was like, 'I've just got to make contact now.' What a day."

The next day, Judge swatted a solo shot off Jake Odorizzi in the Yankees' 12–3 loss to Tampa Bay. He became the second Yankee to homer in each of his first two major-league games. The first to accomplish this feat was Joe Lefebvre, who homered on May 22 and 23, 1980 (the latter as a pinch-hitter). Judge was only two games into his major-league career, but the 24-year-old Californian had already nudged his way into the record books on consecutive days.

IMPACT PLAYER

Aaron Judge's major-league debut got people talking right away. By hitting a home run in his first major-league plate appearance, he didn't just make an impact—he made history. The home run he hit off Tampa Bay Rays right-hander Matt Andriese was a no-doubter the moment it left the bat. The towering drive traveled 457 feet, making it the fourth-longest home run ever hit at the new Yankee Stadium, behind Raul Ibanez (477 feet), Alex Rodriguez (460 feet), Carlos Correa (459 feet), and tied with Mark Trumbo (also 457 feet).

With the homer, Judge became just the third player to hit a ball off or over the glass panels above Monument Park, joining Seattle's Russell Branyan in 2009 and Houston's Carlos Correa in 2016. "That thing was hit a ton," teammate Tyler Austin said of Judge's monstrous shot. "I was really excited for him. It's not every day that you get to do something like that."

The Baseball Hall of Fame requested the bat Judge used during the game, but the Yankees rookie wasn't ready to part with his bat just yet. He said he planned on sticking with the bat until it broke or when he started to feel uncomfortable with it.

Promising Future

The Yankees swept out the old and welcomed the new, and it was the future that stole the show. The promotion of Judge and Austin to the big-league club reunited them with fellow prospect Sanchez, the 23-year-old catcher who had been their teammate at Scranton/Wilkes-Barre and who had beaten them to the Bronx, arriving in early August. Judge definitely felt welcomed in the Yankees clubhouse from the start. During the summer, he became the team's self-appointed disc jockey. Postgame music is common in minor-league locker rooms, but the Yankees' dressing area was quiet. That's until he began picking postgame tunes to play, and it soon became part of the clubhouse culture of the "Baby Bombers."

Judge had an emphatic introduction to the big leagues. He homered in each of his first two games. Then, in his third major-league game, he drove in the lone run in a 1–0 victory over the Toronto Blue Jays when he laced a double to the right-center field gap off the knuckleballer R. A. Dickey. His double, combined with his home runs in each of his first two games, made him the first player in American League history to record at least one extra-base hit and drive in at least one run in each of his first three career games. In those games, Judge was 5-for-10 with two homers and three runs batted in, yet he remained thoroughly unimpressed with himself. "It's still the same game," he said. "You have to try to go out there and have fun."

There seemed to be a greater degree of enthusiasm in the Yankees' dugout with the influx of young, exuberant talent that contributed in meaningful ways. The victory over Toronto was New York's fifth in the past six games and moved the club within five and a half games of the first-place Jays. It also put the Yankees four and a half games behind the Boston Red Sox for the second American League wild-card spot, giving fans something bigger to think about over the final seven weeks of the season.

With nine wins in 15 games since the August 1 trade deadline, the future held the sort of promise that had been missing most of the year. It also gave some credence to management's insistence that it had not punted on the season by parting ways with so many veterans in favor of playing the kids. One in particular, Sanchez, produced an epic final two months, smashing 20 homers, to pace the resurgence. The Yankees went 33-25 in the season's final two months, climbed back into contention, and stayed mathematically alive in the American League wild-card race until the final day of September. New York's faster-than-anticipated youth movement helped to keep the club's postseason hopes alive for 2016 and positioned the Yankees for even more success the next season and beyond.

CHAPTER 6

PROFESSIONAL UPS AND DOWNS

AARON JUDGE LOOKED like he would be the next big thing. In his major-league debut, he whacked a jaw-dropping home run far over the center field wall at Yankee Stadium, announcing his arrival. The next day he hit another titanic homer. It was a fairy-tale beginning. His initial seven-game stint in New York produced eight hits in 26 at-bats and six runs batted in. Unfortunately, the magic soon faded, as he struggled to adjust to major-league pitching. He scuffled for the rest of the season, getting just seven hits over his next 58 at-bats with only two more home runs and 42 strikeouts.

The 2016 season ended for Judge on September 13, due to a muscle strain to his right abdominal oblique. He wound up with a paltry .179 batting average in 27 games played, with just six extra base hits. Most disturbing were the whopping 42 strikeouts in 95 plate appearances, an alarming 44-percent strikeout rate. At one point, he struck out 35 times in 59 at-bats. "Strikeouts were a big concern," said Yankees general manager Brian Cashman.

That was the kind of performance scouts had feared in the run-up to the 2013 draft.

Size Matters

There is a reason Judge was such an enigma as a college baseball player, why he stayed on the draft board until the Yankees picked him 32nd. It wasn't because of his body of work at Fresno State—but his body, period. At 6-foot-7 and 282 pounds, Judge is among the biggest players in baseball history. While tall pitchers are not uncommon, position players the size of Judge rarely last in the majors. High strikeout rates tend to plague the bigger men. "You don't see guys his size get an extended period of time in the big leagues," said Cashman. "The list is very small."

Only 12 hitters in major-league history 6-foot-6 or taller have reached 1,000 career plate appearances. The former Yankees outfielder Dave Winfield is the only one who had a Hall of Fame career. Winfield stood at 6-foot-6 and 220 pounds—one inch shorter and 60 pounds lighter than Judge. In a 22-year career, including nine with the Yankees, Winfield was a 12-time All-Star and seven-time Gold Glove Award winner for fielding excellence. He was elected to the Baseball Hall of Fame in 2001.

Leading up to the draft, some teams were scared away from Judge simply due to the historical reality that very few players his size have successful baseball careers. He appears to be built more like an NBA power forward or an NFL tight end than a fleet-footed outfielder. It's why 29 other teams passed on a massive college prospect with once-in-a-generation power.

To put Judge's size in perspective, LeBron James, the four-time NBA Most Valuable Player, is 6-foot-8 and 250 pounds. Judge is just one inch shorter but weighs thirty pounds more than the three-time NBA Finals champion. And Judge would be a massive tight end, even by NFL standards. Rob Gronkowski, who won two Super Bowls starring at that position for the New England Patriots, is 6-foot-6 and 265 pounds. Judge is one inch taller and 15 pounds heavier than Gronk. It's why people look at Judge and wonder why he isn't playing football.

His unique combination of size, speed, and raw power are matched only by a special few. From the Yankees' point of view, his elite athleticism made him an incomparable prospect, worthy of a first-round draft pick. Among today's stars, only Miami's Giancarlo Stanton, who is 6-foot-6 and 245 pounds, rivals Judge as a physical specimen, which leads the Yankees to believe they have found a special player. It took Stanton only four and a half seasons to become the most prolific home-run hitter in Marlins' franchise history.

While Judge considers it an honor to be compared to the monumental Marlins' slugger, he realizes he has to be his own man. "Trying to be [Giancarlo] Stanton, I can't do that," he said. "I'm just trying to be the best Aaron Judge I can be every day. That's all I can do."

MULTI-SPORT STAR

Dave Winfield was a star baseball and basketball player at the University of Minnesota, where he helped lead the Golden Gophers to their first Big Ten basketball championship in over 50 years, in 1972. He earned All-America and Most Valuable Player accolades as a pitcher in the College World Series during his senior year.

In 1973, Winfield was drafted in three major sports: baseball (by the San Diego Padres), basketball (by the Atlanta Hawks in the NBA and the Utah Stars in the ABA), and football (by the Minnesota Vikings). Winfield was such an astonishing athlete that the Vikings drafted him despite the fact he never played college football.

Winfield wisely chose the Padres baseball team and never spent a day in the minor leagues. He played in nearly 3,000 big-league games, logging 3,110 career hits, 465 homers, and 1,833 runs batted in. And in 1992, at age 41, his 11th-inning two-run double in Game 6 of the World Series won a championship for the Toronto Blue Jays.

Finding Balance

Judge was an instant smash in August 2016. That is, until he wasn't. Seven hits in his first five major-league games were followed by eight hits—total—in his remaining 22 games. He finished with nearly three times as many strikeouts (42) as hits (15), leading many to wonder whether he could make the transition to the majors. No one questioned his work ethic, but scouts questioned his ability to make consistent contact due to his tall frame and long swing. He simply didn't look ready for the big time.

No matter the talent, no matter the expectations, there are no can't-miss prospects in baseball. It seems every year a new player is overhyped and the excitement doesn't match the major-league production. What can be measured in a young athlete, however, is how hard a player works. Judge is a player the Yankees executives raved about for his leadership qualities, his charisma, and his extreme effort. Judge talks like a guy who is aware of the hype, but not intoxicated by it. "One guy can't win a ballgame," he said. "That's always been my mind-set. It takes nine guys. Having the team be my main focus has always been my main focus."

Athletes, especially baseball players, have to deal with low points constantly. Baseball is a game of frustration and failure in many ways. A hitter making an out seven out of 10 times still boasts a solid .300 batting average. In no other sport will a 30-percent success rate get you into the Hall of Fame. Baseball players must learn to accept failure as being part of the game. "If you're not humble," Derek Jeter told young players, "this game will humble you."

Judge understands that baseball is a difficult game to play and a hard psychological grind. "You can't just enjoy the positives," he said. "You've got to enjoy the negatives. I don't like going 0 for 7. I don't like striking out—no one does—but you can't have the good without the bad. The most important thing is when you have those bads, make sure you learn from them. Don't come in [the dugout] and slam your helmet and start cussing. Because the game's not going to stop."

With all this in mind, when answering his critics and doubters, Judge rejects the notion that his size is a disadvantage. "Everything's the same. I'm just bigger than everybody else," he said. "The strike zone may be taller, because I'm taller, but it's what I'm used to. I've had the same strike zone since I was a kid. This is my body; this is my strike zone. I make the same adjustments everyone else does."

TALE OF THE TAPE

In all, only eight players 6-foot-6 or taller have topped 100 career home runs in the major leagues. At the top of list is Dave Winfield, with 465 homers. Next is Adam Dunn, nicknamed "Big Donkey" thanks to his 6-foot-6, 285-pound frame, with 462 career home runs—but he also struck out at an epic rate, logging 2,379 whiffs in 2,001 regular season games. Frank Howard smacked 382 homers over a 16-year career, leading the American League, in 1968

(44) and 1970 (44) with the Washington Senators. Hondo stood 6-foot-7 and was also called the Washington Monument.

Richie Sexson played for five teams during a 12-year career. The 6-foot-7 standout hit 30 homers six times, reaching 40 twice, on his way to 306 career longballs and two All-Star appearances. The 6-foot-8 Tony Clark was a fairly productive first baseman too. He rapped out 251 homers during his 15 seasons with six different teams. Now he is the executive director of the Major League Baseball Players Association.

66

Everyone has something they're always working on."

—Aaron Judge

Career Crossroads

During the winter offseason of 2016, Judge had an epiphany. He realized a man with his strength does not have to hit every ball perfectly square. A homer is a homer, no matter how many rows deep it goes, and he finally came to understand that he did not have to swing wildly to club baseballs over the wall. He flew to New York in January and spent three days at Yankee Stadium taking private lessons from the team's hitting coach Alan Cockrell, tinkering with and refining the mechanics of his swing. And what a mighty swing it is. Judge is not some muscle-bound oaf who clubs baseballs over the fence with brute strength. His swing, from start to finish, has been built as a result of countless hours of repetition to develop a technique that has allowed his rare physical gifts to flourish.

Judge, who sports number 99 and wears high socks, starts at the plate by digging his right foot into the back of the batter's box. His left foot ends up a bit wider than shoulder length and about two inches backward, giving him an open stance. Standing open to the pitcher allows him to see the oncoming pitch with both eyes. Judge took Cockrell's advice and now stands slightly farther off the plate than he did in the minor leagues. This helps to prevent him from getting tied up by inside fastballs while still being able to reach pitches on the outer half of the plate, due to his mammoth wingspan of nearly seven feet.

He stands statue-still at the plate, like his own monument. As the ball travels toward him, Judge loads his weight on his back leg, storing power there. Then there is the leg kick, what Cockrell called a timing mechanism. "All hitters want this," said the hitting guru. "They want to have good timing, and they need to have a good read on the pitch." At the coach's suggestion Judge reduced his leg kick, which kept his head still, to better see the pitched balls. That helps with pitch recognition and with strike zone identification. He was always a patient hitter; he just needed to do a better job of identifying which pitches to let go and which pitches he could brutalize to the bleachers.

The most significant change in Judge's approach to hitting was making better use of the lower half of his body. He focused on being anchored on his back leg, where he could not only achieve good balance in his stance, but also fuel the driving force when he unleashed his swing. As a result of being cemented on his right leg, his head had less movement, which helped him to recognize pitches—be it the spin on a four-seam fastball or a breaking pitch that swerved off the plate.

Spring Fever

Baseball prepares for the regular season in February and March by playing in Florida's Grapefruit League and Arizona's Cactus League. No matter which team is your favorite, there's always an exciting feeling of hope during spring training because everyone believes, deep down, that this could be the year his or her team wins the World Series.

Florida baseball in March is a much more intimate experience than anything you'll find up north during the regular season. George M. Steinbrenner Field in Tampa, Florida, is the place the Yankees call home for their Grapefruit League season, which begins annually in early March. (The Yankees' previous spring training site was in Fort Lauderdale, Florida, from 1962 to 1995.)

Steinbrenner Field is a terrific venue for watching the games. Opened in 1996 originally as Legends Field, it was renamed to honor team owner George Steinbrenner in 2008. The stadium seats 11,076, making it the largest spring training facility in the Grapefruit League. Once the major-league club breaks camp and begins the regular season, the complex also serves as the home of the minor-league Single-A Tampa Yankees of the Florida State League.

As fans enter the complex, the first thing they see is an exhibit displaying the Yankees' retired numbers, just like at Monument Park. Fans will also notice another link to the Bronx. The field's dimensions are an exact replica of Yankee Stadium, measuring 318 feet down the left field line, 408 feet to center field, and 314 feet down the right field line.

Judge arrived in Tampa for spring training workouts in March 2017 with a point to prove. The Yankees had pitted him against another former top prospect, 27-year-old Aaron Hicks, who didn't live up to his perceived potential with the Minnesota Twins before coming to New York in a trade. The two Aarons came to Florida to duel in the sun for the starting right field job. Judge did not shy away from the challenge. "There should always be competition," he said, sounding more like a mature veteran and not like a guy with just 27 major-league games under his belt. "If you are a 10-year veteran, you should not feel comfortable. The unknown is what drives me."

Many considered it Judge's job to lose, especially after Hal Steinbrenner, the team's owner, said during the winter his expectation was for Judge "to be my starting right fielder this year." Still, there are no promises, and having guaranteed job security wasn't Judge's mentality heading into spring training. "I feel like an underdog," he said. "I was in the big leagues for a month, and I got hurt. Now, I'm trying to prove something and win the spot."

Proving Ground

It certainly didn't take long for Judge to build a good case for himself. On the first day of camp, in his second at-bat of the spring, the young right fielder provided a highlight reel moment for the nightly news. With one out, nobody on base, and New York up 1–0 on the Philadelphia Phillies in the bottom of the fifth, Judge stepped up to the plate against left-hander Elniery Garcia and absolutely unloaded on a ball, crushing a solo home run nearly all the way out of Tampa's George M. Steinbrenner Field. Judge's moonshot landed in the deepest park of the park, 449 feet away, and if it weren't for the scoreboard it slammed into, the ball might have gone out of the stadium entirely. To the delight of the Yankees and their fans, it was a sign of things to come.

Judge unveiled a retooled batting stance and a new approach to hitting and showed why he was an improved player. He went deep into counts without swinging at pitchers' pitches, and he also did a better job identifying breaking balls before committing to swing. Yankees manager Joe Girardi said, "it was a very tough call" between the young, right-handed slugger and the switch-hitting Hicks. By batting .344 (21-for-61) with four home runs and cutting down on his strikeouts (13 total), "Judge won the competition and he's our right fielder," said Girardi. "The plan is to play him every day." One person who was not surprised by Judge's transformation was minor-league teammate Rob Refsnyder, who worked out with Judge over the winter and could see a new approach evolving. "I noticed a huge difference in his swing," Refsnyder said.

Judge made the New York Yankees' Opening Day roster as the everyday right fielder, edging out Hicks and getting the nod for the starting job. He broke camp and traveled up north with the major-league team for the first time in his professional career. It was easy to imagine the Yankees rookie becoming one of the biggest stars in New York. But the spotlight does not blind Judge. "Nothing really changes," he said of winning the job. "Now the real work starts."

CHAPTER 7
ROOKIE SENSATION

OPENING DAY FOR the 2017 season was a time of high hopes and great expectations for Aaron Judge. Back in March, when playing opportunities for the rebuilding New York Yankees were an open competition, the primary battle took place in right field, where it was one Aaron versus another—Judge versus Hicks. Both were former first-round draft picks who possessed elite talent but also had enough shortcomings to prompt concern over whether they would ever flourish in the big leagues.

Having won the right field competition over Hicks coming out of spring training, Judge struggled a bit when the games really counted. By the fourth game of the season, Hicks was inserted into the starting lineup in place of Judge, who at the time was 2-for-15 with five strikeouts. After his one-game benching, Judge was back in the starting lineup on April 9 against the Baltimore Orioles in Camden Yards, hoping to jump-start his season. With the Yankees losing the first two games in Baltimore, he picked a perfect time to make an impact and help himself in the process.

Breaking Out

Ever since the season started, Judge had been in a funk at the plate. Following his day off, he remained mired in a 0-for-11 slump. Entering the game against the Baltimore Orioles on April 9, the Yankees were in last place and he was batting .133 with just one run batted in. After a walk and a groundout, he came to the plate in the sixth inning and snapped his oh-for-streak with a laser shot line-drive single that caromed off the base of the left field wall with such force that he didn't dare try for second base. It was the hardest hit ball by a Yankee in the past two seasons, measured at almost 116 miles per hour. Trailing by a run, Judge led off the eighth inning and crushed a fastball from reliever Mychal Givens into the left field seats to tie the score at 3–3. The booming shot was his first homer of the season. "The first one is always the toughest," he said. "I was just glad to make contact and get on base."

The Yankees piled on four more runs in the ninth inning for a 7–3 win. The game ended when Judge made a diving catch on his belly on the dirt of the warning track. With a series sweep averted, he jogged toward his outfield teammates to join the usual celebration. But as he approached them for what looked like a three-way flying chest bump, the others suddenly had second thoughts. Maybe running headlong into a collision with Judge wasn't such a good idea. So as he came charging in, they peeled away, leaving him to connect with nothing but air.

Afterward, Judge laughed at their failed postgame choreography. "I go in there a little aggressively," he said smiling. He probably had some extra energy, riding the high of a two-hit game that included a tying homer in the eighth inning and a run-scoring groundout during the Yankees' four-run ninth. The comeback victory triggered an eight-game winning streak that saw the Yankees move up in the American League East division standings from last place to first place. Judge hit three more homers during the streak and knocked in a total of 10 runs.

The Chicago White Sox snapped the winning streak on April 18, but the Yankees beat them, 9–1, the next day. In the fifth inning, Judge blasted a towering 448-foot homer off Chicago's Dylan Covey about five rows short of the flagpoles behind Yankee Stadium's left-center field bleachers. "He hit that one to the moon," said teammate Chase Headley. The impressive blast was hit off a curveball, thrown at 78 miles per hour, and it left Judge's bat with an exit velocity of 115.5 miles per hour, the largest discrepancy between pitch speed and exit velocity ever recorded. It's one thing to turn a 99-mile-per-hour fastball into a hard-hit ball, but Judge has proven he can do it all by himself.

BIG BANG THEORY

Ever wonder how fast the ball comes off the bat of baseball's fiercest sluggers? Statcast, a state-of-the-art tracking technology, is capable of measuring previously unquantifiable aspects of the game.

Set up in all 30 major-league ballparks, Statcast collects data using a series of high-resolution optical cameras along with radar equipment. The technology precisely tracks the location and movements of the ball and every player on the field, resulting in an unparalleled amount of information covering everything from the spin rate of a pitched ball to the batter's launch angle to the baserunner's acceleration to an outfielder's route efficiency.

As it relates to hitters, Statcast is capable of measuring the velocity, launch angle, and vector of the ball as it comes off the bat. From there, Statcast can also track the hang time and distance that a ball travels, as well as a projected landing-point distance on home runs.

Exit velocity is defined as the speed of a batted ball after a batter hits it. This includes all batted events—hits, outs, and errors. Attaining a high exit velocity is one of a hitter's primary goals. A hard-hit ball won't always have a positive result, but the defense has less time to react, so the batter's chance of reaching base is higher.

Going, Going, Gone!

As a team the Yankees reversed course after a slow start, got their act in gear, and won 10 of their first 15 games for a share of first place. Then they took the Aaron Judge show back on the road, for a game in Pittsburgh, on April 22. The Yankees were leading the Pirates, 10–5, in the ninth inning. Antonio Bastardo entered the game in relief to try keeping the Yankees at bay. He got ahead in the count 1-2, but hitters like Judge only need one mistake to do damage. The left-hander's next pitch came into Judge's wheelhouse, and the slugger unloaded a cannon shot into the second deck of the left-center field seats at Pittsburgh's PNC Park. "I'm not so sure I saw it land," said manager Joe Girardi. "Sometimes these balls [are] hit so far, I just can't follow them."

The Pirates quickly announced that Judge's titanic blast had traveled 457 feet, the longest by a visiting player at PNC Park. Did he get all of it? "I got enough," he said with a smile. It was enough to impress another towering outfielder in Yankees lore. Judge was taken aback when informed that Dave Winfield had re-tweeted a video of his homer. "Dave Winfield? That's pretty cool," said Judge, who now had six homers in 16 games. "Never in my life would I have ever thought that Winfield would be re-tweeting one of my swings."

Aaron Judge takes batting practice before the 2015 Futures Game at Great American Ballpark, in Cincinnati, Ohio. The Futures Game pits the best minor league prospects from the United States against a team of prospects from other countries. (By Arturo Pardavila III from Hoboken, NJ, USA [CC BY 2.0 (http://creativecommons .org/licenses/by/2.0)], via Wikimedia Commons)

Judge was rated by *Baseball America* as the Yankees' top position prospect when he participated in his first big league spring training camp in March 2015.

Judge homered in his first ever exhibition game, impressing teammate Tyler Wade (center). Even so, Judge was assigned to the Trenton Thunder, the Yankees Double-A team, when spring training camp broke.

(Photos by Associated Press)

Judge receives advice from New York Yankees manager Joe Girardi during spring training in 2015. Two years later, Girardi would compare Judge's demeanor and quiet confidence to that of Derek Jeter.

Judge, who possesses impressive skills as an outfielder, is seen here making a diving catch against the Baltimore Orioles in Sarasota, Florida, on March 10, 2015. With terrific range and a strong, accurate throwing arm, Judge has made several eye-popping plays, proving his value as a defender.

(Photos by Associated Press)

Judge waits his turn for batting practice at the Yankees spring training complex in Tampa, Florida, in February 2016. By season's end he would be the International League's top home run hitter and be named to the Triple-A All-Star team.

In 93 games with the Scranton/Wilkes-Barre RailRiders in 2016, Judge boasted a .270 batting average, 19 home runs, and 65 runs batted in. Following the season he was named the International League's "Best Power Prospect."

(Photos by Associated Press)

Judge shares a laugh with Tyler Austin, at right, in the Yankees dugout prior to their major league debut, on August 13, 2016.

Judge and Austin, at right, with the handshake perfected while teammates on the Scranton/Wilkes-Barre RailRiders. The two were called up to the major leagues together.

(Photos by Associated Press)

Judge in the batter's box for the first time in a major league game, on August 13, 2016. He hit a home run off Tampa Bay Rays right-hander Matt Andriese.

Teammates celebrate Judge's first major league hit, a home run that traveled 457 feet over the centerfield wall at Yankee Stadium. At that time it was the fourth-longest home run ever hit at the new ballpark.

(Photos by Associated Press)

Judge and Tyler Austin (26) celebrate New York's 8-4 win over Tampa Bay in their major league debuts, on August 13, 2016.

Judge and Austin (right) meet the press after they hammered back-to-back home runs in the second inning and became the first teammates to hit home runs in their first major league at-bats in the same game.

(Photos by Associated Press)

In May 2017, the Yankees unveil "The Judge's Chambers," a cheering section in the lower level of the right field seats at Yankee Stadium. It features faux wood paneling to resemble a courtroom's jury box.

Fans seated in "The Judge's Chambers" wear black judges' robes emblazoned with the Yankees logo and wield foam gavels.

(Photos by Associated Press)

Judge hits his first career grand slam off Oakland Athletics pitcher Andrew Triggs during the third inning of a 9-5 win in Yankee Stadium, on May 28, 2017.

Judge high fives Ronald Torreyes (74), who is 5'8" and 150 pounds, after Judge's grand slam. Afterward, when a team official asks if he wants the ball retrieved, Judge said no, let the fan keep it.

(Photos by Associated Press)

Judge reaches first base on a free pass in a game against the Kansas City Royals at Yankee Stadium on May 23, 2017. He is the first rookie to reach 100 walks since 1953.

"He's worth the price of admission just to come see him play in person for nine innings," New York Yankees teammate Brett Gardner (11) says of Judge.

Judge's popularity stems from his willingness to sign autographs and interact with fans, and his popularity is growing outside of the Bronx, too.

(Photos by Associated Press)

Judge watching his 29th home run of the season, on July 5, 2017, equaling the New York Yankees single-season rookie record set by Joe DiMaggio in 1936.

Judge smashes DiMaggio's 81-year-old rookie record with home run number 30, a 432-foot blast off Milwaukee's Josh Hader, on July 7, 2017.

(Photos by Associated Press)

Judge (far right) along with Yankees teammates (from left to right) Dellin Betances, Luis Severino, and Starlin Castro, showing off their American League All-Star jerseys at Yankee Stadium, on July 9, 2017.

Judge holds court with the media during the All-Star festivities at Miami's Marlins Park, on July 10, 2017. He was the American League's top vote-getter.

Judge competes in the 2017 Home Run Derby. For weeks, the league office had been pleading for him to enter the showcase event.

Judge hit 47 total homers during the 2017 Home Run Derby, much to the delight of his costumed fans, many of whom wear long white cotton wigs.

(Photos by Associated Press)

Judge celebrating with his Yankees All-Star teammates during the 2017 Home Run Derby.

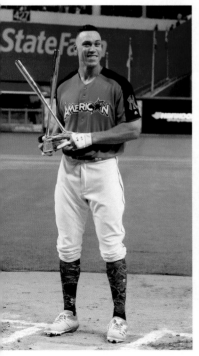

(above) All eyes focus on Judge as he takes the field as a first-time All-Star.

(left) Judge holds the trophy after winning the Home Run Derby in Miami, on July 10, 2017.

(Photos by Associated Press)

Customized jerseys with nicknames, like the ones worn by Judge and Jacoby Ellsbury (22), were donned in celebration of MLB Players Weekend from August 25 to 27, 2017.

Fans all rise whenever Judge jogs over to the outfield wall to give a baseball to an adoring fan.

(Photos by Associated Press)

During the summer of 2017, Aaron Judge was leading the American League in home runs and the major leagues in jersey sales. Fans flocked to the ballparks just to get a glimpse of him.

Judge rounds the bases after hitting his 40th home run of the season, against the Texas Rangers on September 10, 2017, becoming just the second rookie in MLB history to hit at least 40 homers in a season, since Mark McGwire's 49 in 1987.

(Photos by Associated Press)

Judge was a one-man wrecking crew against the Baltimore Orioles in 2017. In 19 games against the Orioles, he went 26 for 61 (.426) with 11 home runs, 24 RBIs, 31 runs scored, and 24 walks.

Judge celebrates with Gary Sanchez, at left, after clouting his 50th home run of the season, on September 25, 2017. Judge became the first rookie to hit 50 homers in a season, breaking Mark McGwire's 1987 rookie record of 49, with Oakland.

Damon Oppenheimer, the Yankees' vice president and director of amateur scouting, presents Judge with a Waterford Crystal "gavel" for breaking Joe DiMaggio's franchise rookie record for home runs, on October 1, 2017. Judge ended the year with 52 homers.

(Photos by Associated Press)

Soon other legends in the Yankees universe took notice. Reggie Jackson hit 563 home runs, won five World Series titles, called himself "the straw that stirs the drink," backed it up, had a candy bar named after him, and owns a Hall of Fame plaque at a baseball museum in Cooperstown, New York. Jackson has known Judge since high school. He also knows a thing or two about launching a baseball into orbit. He earned the nickname "Mr. October" icing the Yankees' 1977 World Series title with three home runs in the deciding Game 6. In an interview, Jackson compared Judge to the likes of modern baseball's most imposing sluggers such as Hank Aaron, Roberto Clemente, Willie Stargell, and Willie McCovey and that the rookie outfielder had the potential to become "the next great Yankee."

Judge was promoted in the lineup from the seventh spot to the heart of the batting order. The offense now revolved around a rookie hitting from the three hole. Judge's can-do attitude emanated from both the batter's box and the dugout. Even after he hit monster home runs, he never put himself above the team. After he blasted a 448-foot home run against Chicago, a reporter from the YES Network asked Judge if he was surprised by his own power. "I'm just trying to make contact, swing at the right pitches," he said in typical Judge fashion. "If I can do that, good things will happen."

Judge's muted reaction to hitting such a long home run corresponded to his motto on Twitter: "If what you did yesterday still seems big today, then you haven't done anything today!"

I'm just trying to make contact. If I do, good things will happen."

—Aaron Judge

Power Surge

The winter of work to minimize his leg kick and improve his batting technique garnered positive results. After homering against the Red Sox at Boston's Fenway Park on April 25, he was the team leader with seven home runs and 15 runs batted in—in just 64 at-bats. Equally impressive was that Judge struck out only 18 times, an acceptable swing and miss percentage for a power hitter. "I think he's always been a fairly patient hitter," said Girardi, "and he made some adjustments in the last couple weeks of spring training that really got him going."

There seemed no stopping Judge now. On April 28, he homered twice to help the Yankees in a comeback victory over the Orioles, a game in which Baltimore blew a 9–1 lead. He belted a solo shot in the fifth inning and a two-run homer in the sixth of a 14–11 Yankees win in 10 innings. His blast in the sixth off Baltimore's Kevin Gausman had an exit velocity of 119.4 miles per hour, the hardest-hit home run of the Statcast era. The ball left his bat looking like a hard-hit single, traveling at a maximum height of 58 feet, and had enough momentum to carry 414 feet from home plate into the grandstand.

The next day, Judge hit his 10th home run of the season in just 21 games, a two-run blast to right-center field in the seventh inning off left-hander Jayson Aquino. The homer tied the major-league record for rookies in the month of April. The big-swinging outfielder, who teammate Matt Holliday has called "Probably the most gifted baseball player I think I've ever been around," joined Colorado's Trevor Story (10 homers in 2016) and Chicago's José Abreu (10 in 2014) in reaching the mark.

His biggest highlight before his homer came in the fourth inning when he recorded the first stolen base of his career. With runners on first and second, he noticed Orioles starter Ubaldo Jiménez wasn't paying attention to him, so he took off and stole third base. Such opportunistic baserunning was a hallmark of a heads-up player, and Judge possessed the natural baseball instincts to make things happen with his legs. But it was in the batter's box with his muscular arms where he did the most damage.

When Judge gets his pitch, more times than not, there will be a loud crack when the horsehide of the baseball meets the 35-inch, 33-ounce Chandler wood bat he wields. Usually, that baseball will travel very far, very fast. He was riding a power surge and creating an electric atmosphere around himself and the team, all while playing a stellar right field. "We knew he was a good outfielder, we knew he could run the bases," said Girardi. "But we wanted the consistent contact, because if a man that size makes consistent contact," he added, "if he gets the barrel of the bat to the ball, he's going to do a lot of damage."

The Yankees finished April sizzling, winning 17 of the final 20 games of the month, and outscoring opponents by more than 50 runs over that span. Judge had an April to remember, with 10 homers, 20 runs batted in, and a .303 average, enabling the Yankees' offense to thrive. The Bronx Bombers shot up in the division standings, from fourth place to first place, in what most fans had accepted as a rebuilding year. Now those fans were dreaming of a long postseason run for their team, and possibly even them bringing a World Series trophy back to the Bronx for the first time since 2009.

SPECIAL GIFTS

How did you spend your birthday in 2017? Aaron Judge celebrated his 25th birthday at Boston's Fenway Park, on April 26.

To get the party started, in the second inning he connected on a fastball from reigning Cy Young Award winner Rick Porcello and went the opposite way over the short right field wall for his seventh homer of the season. Hitting a two-run homer in his first at-bat ever at storied Fenway Park showed he harbored no signs of fear for the Green Monster, and he dominated on both sides of the ball.

In the third inning, with a man on second base, Xander Bogaerts hit a flyball that drifted toward the seats along the right field foul line. Judge, who has excellent speed for such a big man, ran a long way to chase it. He extended his glove arm to make the catch before barreling over the wall and plunging headfirst into the stands. Judge is so rock solid that when he ran into the Fenway wall, manager Joe Girardi said he was concerned for the wall.

The fearless catch while outstretched before tumbling into the crowd was reminiscent of a famous Derek Jeter grab against the Red Sox at Yankee Stadium, in 2004.

CHAPTER 8

RARIFIED AIR

GIVING NEW MEANING to the term huge hit, Aaron Judge's 10 home runs during the month of April averaged 413 feet, and three of his homers measured at least 440 feet. Yankees manager Joe Girardi thought Judge could hit a ball that reached the flagpoles deep beyond the visitors' bullpen at Yankee Stadium. "I think he has a chance to get it there, I really do." He nearly did reach the Stars and Stripes during a game against the Toronto Blue Jays, on May 2. Judge smashed two home runs; one, a no-doubter, catapulted off the bat into restricted airspace and landed in rarely reached parts of the Yankee Stadium bleachers, 391 feet away.

The next day he hit a 435-foot drive for his major-league-leading 13th home run, singled to start the go-ahead rally, and had the first three-hit game of his big-league career, helping the Yankees rally from a four-run deficit to beat the Toronto Blue Jays, 8–6. The two-run shot to straightaway center field in the third inning off Toronto's Marcus Stroman was a good omen. The Yankees' record climbed to 11-0 in games that Judge homered.

Judge went 6-for-12 with three homers and six runs batted in during the three-game series against Toronto. "He's a top-stepper," said Blue Jays outfielder Steve Pearce. "When he goes to the plate, you almost have to stop what you're doing and look."

What a Blast!

When Judge takes batting practice, it is nearly impossible to look away. Routinely, he smashes balls beyond the 408-foot center field wall at Yankee Stadium and high up the 35- to 40-foot rectangular glass batter's eye behind it. In Toronto's Rogers Centre, he blasted one an estimated 510 feet. In Chicago's Guaranteed Rate Field, he blasted another an estimated 504 feet. At Yankee Stadium, he sent a ball soaring into the left field terrace about 475 feet away, obliterating a flat-screen television set located in a concession area. A few weeks later, in Oakland, he knocked two balls into the Plaza Reserve upper level, nearly hitting an unsuspecting fan in the head.

What makes his teammates stop whatever they're doing to catch a glimpse is that when Judge takes a cut, he doesn't look like he's swinging for the fences. His bat smoothly slides through the zone—and then the ball explodes. "He is a freak," said teammate Chase Headley. The swing is a kinetic marvel, and the power generated is simply otherworldly. According to Statcast figures, Judge hits the ball harder than anybody, at a time when technology has been developed to call attention to this. In limited at-bats during his brief 2016 call-up, Judge's average exit velocity of 95.5 miles per hour ranked second in the majors to only Seattle Mariners slugger Nelson Cruz (95.9 mph) among hitters with at least 40 batted balls. It was a sign of things to come.

By May of 2017, he already had hit eight balls in play at a speed of 115 miles per hour or higher. Fans flocked to the ballparks just to get a glimpse of him. When he took batting practice, opposing players stopped their own preparations to watch his every move. Judge was evolving into an individual with great public appeal. "He's worth the price of admission just to come see him play in person for nine innings," said teammate Brett Gardner.

Judge had a league-leading 13 homers in 27 games, including 10 in 15 games. He was having the greatest season of any Yankees rookie since Joe DiMaggio burst onto the scene in 1936. As a rookie left fielder, the 21-year-old DiMaggio, also a Californian, batted .323 with 29 home runs, 125 runs batted in, 206 hits, 44 doubles, and 15 triples, most in the American League. DiMaggio didn't win the Rookie of the Year Award, but then again, it didn't become an official MLB award until 1947.

JOLTIN' JOE

Of all the legendary Yankees' batting records that once seemed unconquerable—Babe Ruth's 714 career home runs and Roger Maris's 61 home runs in a season—only Joe DiMaggio's hitting streak in 1941 has stood the test of time. "Joltin' Joe" hit safely in 56 games in a row.

DiMaggio was among the game's greatest natural right-handed hitters. He could hit for average and hit for power. He had a lifetime batting average of .325 and hit 361 home runs. DiMaggio had a great batting eye for a power hitter, as the numbers suggest: in his 13-year career, he struck out only 369 times. He was the picture of grace in the outfield—not flashy, just knowing where he should be and getting there in plenty of time to make the catch. His manager, Joe McCarthy, called him the best baserunner he had ever seen.

DiMaggio was a winning player. He played on nine World Series championship teams with the Yankees. He won three Most Valuable Player Awards (1939, 1941, and 1947) and was elected to the Hall of Fame in 1955.

MVP! MVP! MVP!

For all his extraordinary April efforts, Judge was named the American League Rookie of the Month. A reporter asked him to describe what his reaction would have been had somebody predicted he'd get off to this kind of hot start. "I would have laughed at them," he said in a self-deprecating way. "I would have said, 'You guys are joking with me.' I just try to come in here and do my work and prepare the right way and do whatever I can to help the team. That's what I'm trying to do." When asked if he'd ever been in this type of zone, Judge balked. "I wouldn't say I'm in the zone. I'm just competing."

For about a decade, Major League Baseball has honored the armed forces by dressing teams in special uniforms during the Memorial Day holiday weekend. Beginning in 2008, teams wore uniforms featuring team and player names and jersey numbers styled in a Stars and Stripes design, as well as caps of red, white, and blue combinations. In 2013, the league transitioned to camouflage. On May 28, Judge and his teammates suited up to play the Oakland Athletics in a specially designed cap and jersey that featured an authentic military digital camouflage design licensed from the United States Marine Corps.

Never one to blend in with his surroundings, Judge was clearly visible to the Yankee Stadium faithful when he found himself up in the third inning with two outs, the bases loaded, and his team trailing by one run. On a 2-1 count, Oakland's sidewinding right-handed pitcher Andrew Triggs left a 90-mile-per-hour fastball over the heart of the plate. Judge swung with an easy motion, and with a flick of his wrists, the ball sailed 376 feet into the right field stands for his first career grand slam. The hometown crowd chanted, "MVP! MVP! MVP!" as he rounded the bases. Afterward, when a team official asked if he wanted the ball retrieved, Judge told him no, let the fan keep it. Judge's homer propelled the Yankees to a 9–5 win. "It was a big momentum-shifter," said Girardi.

The next day, Judge hit his 17th home run of the season, a scream-ing line drive against Dylan Bundy of the Orioles. It landed 429 feet away and broke a tie with Mike Trout for the major-league lead. Two days later, Trout injured his left thumb on a steal of second base and landed on the disabled list for six weeks. The injury also put Judge in position to become the American League's top vote-getter for the All-Star Game.

Judge's offensive breakout came at an especially crucial time. Gary Sanchez had suffered an arm injury a week into the season, and the club desperately needed a dependable power source. The thought of the two young sluggers hitting together once Sanchez returned to form was truly exciting. In the meantime, with a .330 batting average and 27 runs batted in, Judge had emerged as the face of the retooling "Baby Bombers."

Fans chanted "MVP! MVP! MVP!" as he rounded the bases.

In the Spotlight

The law of gravity dictated that Judge was due for a course correction. During the season's second month, he recorded just two round-trippers in 19 games from May 5 to May 27, and his batting average dropped from .337 to .316. Never one to panic, Judge's disarming, easygoing personality was always on display. The Yankees were in first place, a pleasant surprise and ahead of schedule. The team went 10-9 during Judge's mini-slump, but increased its first-place lead from one-half game to two. Visitors to the Yankees clubhouse noticed Judge's quiet leadership was quickly making an impact on the team—not only with his ability to hit a baseball, but also with the way he carries himself. He is too young a player and too new to the big leagues to ever get in teammates' faces, nor would he want to take over the clubhouse with headline-making interviews. He's not wired to seek attention. You wouldn't know from his demeanor during or after a game whether he'd collected three hits or struck out four times.

Said Judge: "You're going to have those times when you go 0-for-20, 0-for-30. It's all about just staying [even-keeled]. For me, it's just baseball. You're going to have times where you get to the plate, and the baseball's going to look like a golf ball up there. And then you're going to have times when you're up there and everything is looking right down the middle. That's baseball."

The rookie still was figuring it all out, and he was able to out-adjust enemy hurlers to maintain the upper hand. By June, the right fielder had already smashed an MLB-best 17 homers, one less than his career total at Fresno State. He also had 37 runs batted in, to go along with an improved .327 batting average, and a cannon of a right throwing arm. He was far and away the favorite for the American League Rookie of the Year, and he was in the conversation about Most Valuable Player too. Judge was a star among stars, so much so that it seemed as if just about every player on the opposing teams was talking about him. At the 2017 All-Star Game festivities, Tampa Bay Rays pitcher Chris Archer was asked whom he sees as the new "face" of the sport. "Right now, it's Judge," he said. "It's special what he's doing, and he's doing it on the biggest possible stage. People already are saying this: he may be the second coming of Derek Jeter."

RISING STAR

It is a rare occurrence for any rookie player to make such a huge impact for his ballclub, and it has been a long time since any rookie player left such a large footprint on the game in such a short period of time. In 2001, Ichiro Suzuki came to play in America for the Seattle Mariners and set the game ablaze. Seattle's new Japanese star led the major leagues in hits and stolen bases, with a .350 batting average tops in the league. Ichiro, who is known by his first name, won a Silver Slugger award and a Gold Glove for his outfield wizardry, as well as a spot on the All-Star team. Even more remarkable, Ichiro won both the Rookie of the Year and league's Most Valuable Player Awards in one season. Only Fred Lynn equaled the milestone while playing for the Boston Red Sox in 1975.

Eventful Week

Judge continued pummeling the ball to help the Yankees win five of their six games against the Red Sox and Orioles and took home Player of the Week honors for the period ending June 11. During that eventful week, he launched a home run that left his bat at 121 miles per hour, breaking his own record, and a day later deposited a ball in the seats 495 feet away. In the final two games of the Baltimore series, he went 7-for-8 with three homers, a pair of doubles, two walks, and six runs batted in. When the dust settled, Judge sat atop the American League leaderboard in home runs (21), runs batted in (47), and batting average (.344), as well as runs (57), walks (40), and total bases (166).

Fresno State head baseball coach Mike Batesole was anticipating Judge's visit to Anaheim, California, for a three-game series, beginning on June 12. The coach spent time watching his former Bulldogs player take batting practice before each game. He said it was special to see Judge in his element. "It was really cool," said Batesole. "I never got to play in the big leagues, but every time one of my guys gets there it feels like a tiny piece of me does."

The New York Yankees were perched in first place atop the American League East standings. With the starting pitching exceeding expectations and a quartet of flamethrowers coming out of the bullpen, the Bronx faithful were confident their team would qualify for the postseason. After a win on June 8 over the Boston Red Sox—in which a healthy Sanchez blasted a pair of 400-foot homers—the Yankees were 34-23 with a three-game lead over their archnemesis.

As the Yankees sprinted into contention, Judge, Sanchez, and Luis Severino led the way, already performing like franchise cornerstones, the kind of players who are expected to be in the Bronx for many years to come. Arguably the most impactful of them all is Judge, a breakthrough star, at 25, in his first full season in the majors, who flexed his muscles and triggered the team's meteoric rise. Amazingly, Judge had become an early contender to do what only one major-league player had done since 1968 and only two Yankees—Lou Gehrig and Mickey Mantle—had ever accomplished: win the Triple Crown by leading the league in batting average, home runs, and runs batted in.

In a year in which the Yankees were not even supposed to be a factor, a new star had emerged in the Bronx. He is a 6-foot-7, 282-pound symbol of the youth movement that has changed the complexion of the New York Yankees. Judge was transforming baseball's marquee franchise back into a legitimate contender and becoming the most celebrated athlete in New York. This was heady stuff for a 25-year-old—especially one who stands out wherever he goes. Yet Judge seemed able to roll with all the attention and have fun without taking his focus off the game. He had already appeared on the cover of *Sports Illustrated* and made guest appearances on several late night television talk shows. Meanwhile, the hits kept on coming, and Judge was completely changing baseball, one big hit at a time.

CHAPTER 9

THE PRIDE OF LINDEN

SEVEN YEARS AFTER spurning the Oakland Athletics' contract offer, Aaron Judge was back at the Oakland Coliseum on June 15, 2017, as baseball's newest superstar. He was leading the major leagues in home runs and ranked second in the American League in batting average and runs batted in. Some 2,000 people from the town of Linden became fixated on the ascendancy of their strapping homegrown hero.

Barely a 90-minute drive from the Bay Area, Linden is full of fans who root for the San Francisco Giants and Oakland Athletics. But Judge's popularity altered the town's allegiances. Pinstriped jerseys and Yankees hats now popped up all around town. Each day, after hitting a ball harder and farther than the day before, the pride of Linden drew nationwide headlines with each mighty swing. When the Yankees visited Oakland to play a four-game series in the Coliseum, most of Linden was expected to be there, having bought up tickets in the right field seats to be as close as possible to their native son. Though the Yankees lost all four games, Judge performed superbly in the second game, going 2-for-3 with a triple and a home run, three RBIs, two walks and two runs scored.

CHARACTER STUDY

It didn't take long for the New York Yankees organization to realize Aaron Judge wasn't just any ordinary prospect: he is as big and agile as an NFL tight end, yet as personable and trusting as he is talented. All teams obsess over character when scouting amateur players. But the Yankees, because of where they play, need players with mental toughness too. The Yankees' franchise, the team's fans, and the local media have cracked many great talents in the past. When it comes to drafting players, there's a much smaller margin for error in the fishbowl of New York City. The Yankees loved Judge's size and swing and athleticism—but they also believed they had found someone gigantic who could handle enormous pressure by thinking small.

Take for instance the game against the Baltimore Orioles when Judge hit a 495-foot home run into the upper stands at Yankee Stadium. That astounding home run, hit on June 11, was the longest ever since the major leagues started recording home-run distances. But when asked about the feat by the Yankees' YES Network television reporter, Judge brushed it off. "It means nothing to be honest," he said. "I'm just glad we came up with a win."

In typical fashion, Judge ended up changing the subject of the conversation, opting instead to talk about the Yankees defense and pitching staff. Forget that Judge also had his first career four-hit game that day. With such a humble attitude off the field and a tenacious work ethic on it, it's fair to say that Judge is more than just the ideal rookie player for any team, in every sport. He has become perhaps an ideal leader for the Yankees in the new post–Derek Jeter era. It's far too early to tell whether Judge will have a career or presence of Jeter's stature, but evidence of his greatness as a player and a teammate is already mounting before the court.

Heady Company

Recently, Yankees manager Joe Girardi made news by publicly comparing Judge to Derek Jeter. There may be something to that comparison in terms of each player's demeanor and quiet confidence. "He is a little bit like Jeter for me," said Girardi. "He has a smile all the time. He loves to play the game. You always think he is going to do the right thing on the field and off the field." A player can receive no higher praise.

Judge's tangible contributions—the tape-measure home runs and sparkling catches in the outfield—are on display for all to see, but he has some intangible traits that do not show up in the box scores. He does something that is very Jeter-esque too. After the final out of each inning, Judge runs in from right field and waits outside the dugout for his fellow teammates. He greets them and allows them to enter the dugout first, offering a kind word of encouragement and often a high-five or pat on the back. He only enters the dugout after all his teammates have returned. This echoed Jeter's enthusiasm for congratulating teammates after big plays, only, it may be better.

"I've always done it, in the minor leagues, too," said Judge. "If someone makes a good play or someone does something on defense, I want to be there and say, 'Hey man, nice play' or 'Good job.' If there is

THE CAPTAIN

Derek Jeter grew up wanting to be the shortstop for the New York Yankees, and his wish came true. "All I ever wanted to be was a Yankee," he is fond of saying. "When I was a kid I was always hoping there'd be a jersey left for me to wear with a single digit."

Jeter played his entire 20-year career in the Bronx (1995–2014). He captained the Yankees during his final 12 seasons, capping a career that included five World Series titles, a .310 batting average, and a New York–record 3,465 hits. A 14-time All-Star, Jeter's personal won-loss record was 511 games above .500, the highest mark by any position player in Major League Baseball history, according to the Elias Sports Bureau.

The team retired his number 2 jersey during a pregame ceremony on May 14, 2017. He is the 22nd player to have his number retired by the Yankees, by far the most among major-league teams. The Yankees also unveiled a plaque for him in the stadium's Monument Park.

miscommunication in the outfield, it gives me a chance to grab them real quick and say something."

Back in Jeter's day, when the Yankees scored or got a big hit, Jeter was always the first out of the dugout to congratulate his teammates. It was a trademark Jeter move. "That's who he was," said Girardi. "Derek was all about winning. I feel the same about that [Judge] kid. It is very genuine. He is all about the team. His encouragement of players, help-ing guys, being upbeat all the time, it is really kind of cool to witness."

Girardi thinks Judge is a leader in his own way despite being a rookie—something that might irk veterans if Judge wasn't so respectful and earnest. "I think he does things, like Derek did, when Derek was young, just by example," said the manager. The top-step move could be seen as grandstanding, if Judge didn't act the right way. "It's genuine," said third baseman Chase Headley. "He is not doing it to have somebody write about it or see it." Teammates notice that he is not trying to stick out, but rather help out. "He is a positive influence on his teammates," said left fielder Brett Gardner. "He always has a positive attitude."

Loyal Roots

Besides being the biggest person in history to play professional baseball, Judge may be the most polite too. He shakes hands when introduced, smiles and looks you in the eye, and sprinkles his conversation with "Please" and "Thank you." He makes a point to remember the names of those covering the team and addresses reporters individually, by name, during interviews. Judge's teammates adore him and are protective of their young slugger. Not that a guy that big needs backup, but they marvel at how well he has handled the media crush of the Big Apple. "He's a big kid, he can't hide," said Girardi. "He's noticed everywhere, yet all he cares about is playing ball. That's what makes him so remarkable."

The instant celebrity hasn't overwhelmed him. Even though Judge could stay out late enjoying New York City's stellar nightlife, he doesn't go out after Yankees games. He keeps his Twitter account G-rated for his 160K-plus followers and said he avoids bars and clubs. "I have a very short window to play this game," he says. "The last thing I want to do is waste it being out on the town. I want to get every ounce I can out of my body."

Judge is a homebody who was adopted at birth by two middle-aged educators in Linden, California. To this day, he remains loyal to those roots. He calls his parents, Wayne and Patty, every day. He sent flowers on Mother's Day. And at the conclusion of the Yankees' last road trip to the West Coast, Judge got a care package from his mom to take back to New York: a batch of chocolate chip cookies.

When Judge calls his parents, baseball isn't the primary subject—a 495-foot home run against the Orioles included. "We don't talk about it much, to be honest," he said. "They say 'Good game,' stuff like that, but that's the last thing I want to do when I call my parents is to talk about more baseball. I want to know how they're doing, how's the dog doing, what did you do today."

Judge said that he speaks with his parents on the telephone every day. On a recent afternoon, hours before a game at Yankee Stadium, he said that he had just hung up the phone with his mom, who had been doing some yard work. "I just thanked her again for everything she's done, and [told] her again I know I wouldn't be in the position I am now if it wasn't for her love and guidance," Judge said, adding, "I wouldn't be a New York Yankee if it wasn't for my mom."

Judge often talks about the influence other people have had on his life long before he'll talk about himself. He credits his respectful demeanor to his parents. Fresno coach Mike Batesole called Judge a special kid who truly cares about other people. You see it every inning, after Judge takes his warmup throws, when he jogs over to the right field stands where admirers scream his name and he gently hands the ball to a young fan. "That can only come from Mom and Dad," said Batesole of Judge's innate kindness. "When it's that deep and that real, that means he was raised right."

66

I wouldn't be a New York Yankee if it wasn't for my mom."

—Aaron Judge

"The Animal"

Incredibly, the young man who avoided being sent back to Triple-A Scranton/Wilkes-Barre by barely winning the right field job out of spring training had now become famously known for the exit velocity off his bat, which measures how hard a player hits a ball. Heading into play on June 8, there had been 34 batted balls that registered an exit velocity of 115 miles per hour or greater in 2017—and Judge was responsible for 11 of them. He also owned the two hardest-hit balls of the season up to that time, a double at Wrigley Field in May and a monster dinger against the Orioles back in April.

Judge decided to go ahead and break his own record again. In the sixth inning of New York's 9–1 win over the Red Sox, the right fielder hit a Fernando Abad fastball so hard it nearly bored a hole in the Earth. Judge's line-drive single up the middle in the sixth inning registered an exit velocity of 120 miles per hour off the bat—the hardest-hit ball in the majors at that point in the season, according to Statcast. The 6-foot-7, 282-pound rookie now held the top three spots on that list. The rest of the majors were stuck on zero. "That is why I call him 'The Animal,'" said catcher Gary Sanchez. "He's amazing."

If one swing of the bat could overshadow a game in which the Yankees scored 14 runs, or completed a three-game series sweep in which they outscored the Baltimore Orioles by 38–8, or rode a five-game winning streak, it was the swing that Judge took against Logan Verrett in the sixth inning of the Yankees' 14–3 win over the visiting Orioles. According to Statcast, Major League Baseball's tracking technology, Judge's blast was 495 feet, the longest in the majors at that point in the season. Verrett's pitch to Judge had arrived at 85 miles per hour. The ball's exit velocity off Judge's bat was 119 miles per hour, and its launch angle was 28.4 degrees. That was not quite in the class of the home run he hit on June 10 off Chris Tillman, which was clocked at 121 miles per hour, the hardest home run ever hit, breaking the record—one that Judge already held. And it reached an altitude of 124 feet, which put it momentarily on a level with, if not above, the façade ringing the top of Yankee Stadium. Only the great Yankees switch hitter Mickey Mantle had ever come close to hitting a fair ball out of Yankee Stadium.

THE MICK

In time, Aaron Judge's 495-foot shot may be ranked with the one Mickey Mantle hit at the old Griffith Stadium in Washington, DC, in 1953, measured at 565 feet, officially the longest home run ever hit. Hitting right-handed, Mantle drilled a rising line drive that nicked the lower right-hand corner of a huge beer sign atop a football scoreboard behind the left-center field bleachers. The ball left the stadium, carried across a street, and landed in the backyard of a home.

This blow was responsible for the expression "tape-measure home run" because the Yankees publicity director, Red Patterson, immediately left the press box, found himself a tape measure, and paced off the distance to the spot where witnesses said the ball came down.

Then there was the one Mantle hit left-handed off Kansas City pitcher Bill Fischer on May 22, 1963—the blast that struck the façade atop the right field upper deck and nearly became the only fair ball ever to exit the old Yankee Stadium. It left his bat at an angle of 27 degrees with a velocity of 124 miles per hour and was one of the hardest-hit balls in history. ESPN's Home Run Tracker projected that it would have traveled 503 feet if it had completed its arc and landed on River Avenue.

CHAPTER 10

ALL-STAR GLORY

AARON JUDGE WAS having an absolutely phenomenal and historic first full season, the type that might be one for the ages, or at least, the record book. His contributions were Rookie of the Year material. And if he stayed on the same attacking pace, especially if the Yankees contended for a postseason berth, it would be very hard to make a case against Judge being named the American League's Most Valuable Player as well. What he was doing was unique and special enough to mark a new era for the sport.

Whether or not he was a shoo-in to win both of those trophies or if the Yankees won the pennant in 2017—much less a 28th World Series title—Judge's work so far had still put him in some legendary Yankees company. He hit home run number 25 on June 22. Only 10 other times since 1901 had a Yankees player hit 25 homers inside the season's first 70 games. Half of these were the work of Babe Ruth, while fellow

Yankees legend Roger Maris had two of them. Lou Gehrig, Mickey Mantle, and Alex Rodriguez had one each. Yet not one of those five famous Yankees, three of them already in the Hall of Fame, hit as many home runs in their rookie year as Judge had already hit by the end of June.

He set a New York Yankees single-season rookie record with 30 home runs, passing Joe DiMaggio's mark of 29 set in 1936. Judge smashed that 81-year-old record with home run number 30—on July 7. He also joined Maris and Rodriguez as the only Yankees to hit at least 30 home runs before the All-Star break. Judge had essentially guaranteed he would be a member of the American League All-Star team. He held the league lead in home runs and was on his way to becoming only the second player in MLB history to capture the single-season home-run crown during a rookie campaign, joining Mark McGwire, who recorded 49 homers for the Oakland Athletics in 1987. The Yankees phenomenon was also a very real Triple Crown threat, as he stockpiled spectacular statistics and compiled incredible numbers that were adding up to a truly monumental season.

I wouldn't be in this position if it weren't for my teammates."

—Aaron Judge

Hero Worship

After surprising much of baseball with a 38-23 start, the New York Yankees crashed to Earth by losing 18 of 25 games heading into the All-Star break. The Yankees were still leading the American League wild card race, thanks to four homegrown prospects who earned spots on the American League All-Star team. Judge, catcher Gary Sanchez, and pitchers Luis Severino and Dellin Betances, and the injured second baseman Starlin Castro, who could not participate, gave the Yankees five total selections, tied for most in the majors. They would be temporarily trading in their pinstripes for fluorescent South-Beach-inspired uniforms when the All-Star Game was played at Marlins Park in Miami, on July 11. "I've got to call my family and tell them to book a flight to Miami," said Judge. "They're going to be excited."

Nobody was more excited than Judge. He grew up a huge fan of the San Francisco Giants and adored the club that won the franchise's first World Series since the Manhattan-based New York Giants won it all in 1954. His favorite player on the 2010 Giants was their then-young catcher, Buster Posey. Seven years later, Posey was in Miami for his fifth All-Star Game, and Judge was there too, as a first-time All-Star. They met for the first time at Marlins Park hours before the Home Run Derby. Judge was awestruck.

"I was coming out of the bathroom, and he was walking in the clubhouse and I just stopped and said, 'Buster, huge fan man,'" he said. "I have fun watching what he's doing, the way he plays on the field and how he acts off the field. He's a true definition of a professional." During their brief conversation, Posey responded to Judge's flattery with a return compliment. "You've been fun to watch," he told Judge. "Keep it going and congrats."

During the first half of the season, Posey had noticed Judge's stats, size, and athletic ability. "I'm jealous," said Posey, who stands 6-foot-1 and weighs 215 pounds. "I was thinking about that the other day. I was watching their game and saw him moving around in right field and was thinking to myself how impressive that is, it's pretty incredible how athletic he is."

Judge mentioned Posey several times during his 45-minute press conference during the afternoon before the derby. He said Posey was the player whom he was most eager to meet when he showed up for his first All-Star Game festivities. "Meeting Buster Posey, that was pretty cool," said Judge. "Just because I grew up a Giants fan and having a chance to meet him and play on the same field with him is pretty cool."

Must See TV

He'd been the most dominant hitter in the majors, with 30 homers at the break. He was also leading the American League with 62 runs batted in, and his .329 batting average was the AL's second-best. In his rookie campaign, Judge was the highest vote-getter for the American League All-Star team, collecting 4,488,702 votes—and for good reason. "It's pretty incredible," he said. "Any time you get [recognized] like this, I feel like it's a team award. If I look back, I wouldn't be in this position if it weren't for my teammates that put me in a good position. I'm always coming up with runners on base. I'm always coming up in big situations to do a job."

He had almost instantly become one of the most captivating players in baseball and the fans' overwhelming favorite to play right field in his first All-Star Game. "He's must-watch TV," said Nationals right fielder Bryce Harper. But first, Judge was the headliner at the Home Run Derby. For weeks, the league office had been pleading for Judge to enter the showcase event. This was far different from the other home-run-hitting contest he entered—the one in Omaha, site of the College World Series, in 2012.

This time, Judge would be trying to unseat the defending champion, Giancarlo Stanton, on his home turf in Miami. The showdown between the hulking hitters promised to be the most sizzling event of the All-Star festivities. The gone-a-thon at Marlins Park was highly anticipated, and the accompanying buzz was reminiscent of heavyweight title fights of the past. It was no surprise that when MLB.com conducted a poll of players to find out which player they most wanted to see in the derby, Stanton and Judge were the resounding winners. It was difficult to recall a more highly hoped-for derby encounter than Stanton and Judge, the top two seeds in an eight-man tournament.

The New York Yankees' breakout star rose to the occasion. In a prolific power display, Judge defeated Minnesota Twins third baseman Miguel Sanó, 11–10, in the final round, claiming the Home Run Derby crown. He hit homers on the first three pitches he saw in the final round and added a 480-foot shot for his fourth homer. With two minutes left in the four-minute regulation round, he blasted a 458-foot shot to straightaway center field for his 11th homer to pass Sanó and end the derby. With less than two minutes remaining on the clock when his final bomb left the building, he certainly had plenty left in the tank. "I had a lot of fun," he said. "I hoped the fans enjoyed the show."

DAZZLING DERBY

Aaron Judge won the Home Run Derby in 2017, putting on the best show in the event since Josh Hamilton of the Texas Rangers dazzled the old Yankee Stadium in 2008. Hamilton made the Bronx faithful swoon with a record-setting first round. Hamilton put on an absolute show with 28 homers—hitting 13 in a row at one point, and 16 of 17, and 20 of 22. Three of Hamilton's homers went 500 feet or more, including one that threatened to pull a Mickey Mantle and hit the façade at the top of the stadium, sending the crowd into a frenzy.

Hamilton's outburst was jaw dropping, but it wasn't enough to claim the top spot. Unfortunately, Hamilton didn't have enough in him in the last round, losing to Minnesota's Justin Morneau, 5–3, despite out-homering him in the derby 35–22. Morneau may have taken home the trophy, but the 2008 derby will always be remembered for Hamilton reaching a dinger nirvana that few could even dream of, as he helped close out the old Yankee Stadium in style.

Show Stopper

Judge's storybook season only kept getting better and better. He added another trophy to his case following his Home Run Derby triumph. Asked the difference between the college and pro derbies, he replied: "A lot more fans. But it was about the same. You're nervous; your adrenaline is pumping. You're excited. This was an incredible experience."

Judge was the first rookie ever to win the Home Run Derby outright. He was also the fourth Yankees player to win the competition, joining Robinson Canó (2011), Jason Giambi (2002), and Tino Martinez (1997). And to think, here's what he said before the event: "I'm just trying to make it out of the first round." Judge did way more than that—with one of the most remarkable performances in the history of the event. After being booed by the Miami crowd, Judge defeated Marlins first baseman and hometown favorite Justin Bour, 23–22, in the first-round matchup. "I was expecting it," Judge said of the jeers. "It was all part of the atmosphere."

The 25-year-old slugging phenom blasted 23 homers to advance, including a 501-foot shot that sailed over the Marlins' home-run sculpture in center field. He also hit a ball off the roof, while going opposite field a few times. "He looks like a contact hitter trapped in an ogre's body," said Colorado's Charlie Blackmon, a derby participant. The 23 homers Judge hit were the third-most ever in a single round. Josh Hamilton hit an MLB-record 28 in 2004, while Giancarlo Stanton (2016) and Bobby Abreu (2005) each hit 24. He averaged 432 feet on his homers in round one with an average exit velocity of 111.9 miles per hour.

Judge's teammate, Gary Sanchez, the number eight seed, unleashed the biggest upset of the tournament, knocking out defending champion and number one seed Stanton in round one, 17–16. The much hyped and hoped for matchup between Stanton and Judge was not to be, but it didn't matter, because Judge simply stole the show.

In round two, he hit three 500-foot homers. His last four swings traveled 504 feet, 513 feet—an absolute bomb off the glass beyond the left field seats—458 feet, and 507 feet. He defeated Los Angeles Dodgers first baseman Cody Bellinger, son of ex-Yankee Clay, 13–12, to advance to the finals. His homers in the second round averaged 448 feet. Judge stayed humble after the win. "I had no pressure. I'm a rookie, and it was my first time doing it," he said. "I had no expectations. I was just going to go out there, have some fun and see what we could do tonight. I had a blast. I enjoyed every minute of it."

The crowd had booed Judge in the early rounds, but by the end of the competition they were cheering him on for his otherworldly display of power. Other players and celebrities took notice of the 25-year-old outfielder that trended across all social media platforms. "Aaron Judge is a beast," tweeted the NBA's Joel Embiid. "The Judge rendered the verdict! HR Derby champ! Congratulations!" tweeted Dave Winfield.

Judge certainly cut an outsize figure as he hit home runs in rapid progression, many of them prodigious blasts. He hit 47 total homers during the derby that traveled 3.9 miles worth of distance—including four that traveled more than 500 feet. Patty and Wayne Judge cheered on their son from the stands. A reporter asked Patty what it was like to see her son becoming a household name in the sport. "My eyes tell you what a parent's pride is," she replied, crying. "My son's actions tell you more about him than I can tell you about him. I'm speechless."

ROOF SHOT

You can't Judge-proof a ballpark. During the Home Run Derby Aaron Judge did what no man had ever done before: he hit a ball off the roof of Miami's Marlins Park. That wasn't ever supposed to happen.

The engineers designing the retractable roof of Marlins Park set out to determine how high the roof would have to be so as not to interfere with balls in play. They studied the air density and temperatures of Miami and plugged those variables into equations from NASA and then applied it to their own algorithm to determine the final shape of the roof structure. The engineers finally arrived at a height of 210 feet above the ground at its apex above second base to make sure no batted ball hit the roof.

Then Judge showed up and hit the roof with a Home Run Derby blast that defied NASA calculations. The Marlins estimated that it cleared one girder and smacked against another at a height off the ground of about 170 feet in deep left-center field. That meant he hit a baseball about 17 stories high in the air with enough power that it traveled about 300 feet. Only the superhuman strength of Judge could make actual rocket scientists from NASA look dumb.

CHAPTER 11

TAKING THE GAME BY STORM

ALL THE MOTIVATION Aaron Judge needs is kept on his cell phone. It's right there on his notes app, always atop the list for quick access. He looks at it every day and said he's done so for months, letting it serve as the perfect provider of perspective. The message reads: .179—an acknowledgment of what he hit last season in his debut with the New York Yankees. "It's motivation to tell you 'Don't take anything for granted,'" said Judge to explain why he keeps the reminder of 2016's struggles with him at all times. "This game will humble you in a heartbeat. So I just try to keep going out there and play my best game every day, because I could hit .179 in a couple of weeks."

That seemed unfathomable in July 2017. Entering the All-Star Game, the Yankees rookie star was leading the majors with 30 home runs, 75 runs scored, a .449 on-base percentage, and a .697 slugging percentage. Each time opponents thought they might have located a hole to exploit, he found a way to counteract their efforts. The massive guy who wasn't even a lock to make the big-league club out of spring training was all set for his All-Star debut at Miami's Marlins Park, on July 11. He was batting third and playing right field for the American League. "He's probably exhausted from all those home runs he hit last night," Yankees reliever Dellin Betances said of Judge.

Playing in his first All-Star Game, here's how Judge's at-bats went: in the first inning, he struck out swinging on a 3-2 slider facing Washington Nationals right-hander Max Scherzer with one out and a runner on first. "I was nervous the first pitch, but after that it's go time. On 3-2 I was getting ready for 100 mph, and I got a slider." In the third inning, he grounded out to shortstop facing St. Louis Cardinals righty Carlos Martínez with a runner on second base and two down. In the fifth inning, he lined out to deep center field with two outs and a runner on first facing Los Angeles Dodgers left-hander Alex Wood, before being replaced in the bottom of the fifth inning.

The American League defeated the National League, 2–1 in extra innings, for its fifth straight win in the Midsummer Classic. Judge left three runners on base but was all smiles in the winning clubhouse. "This was awesome," he said. "My first time coming to Miami, and the goal was to have some fun and compete. That's what happened. We came out with a win. It was just an awesome experience all around. What a day. What a couple of days."

What a year for Judge. What a season. And it was only July.

You don't take anything for granted."

—Aaron Judge

Rookie Wonder

Back on June 11 against Baltimore, Judge shocked the sports world by blasting a home run that landed 495 feet away from home plate. No one in the Yankees dugout could remember seeing anything like it. "Did it go over the bleachers?" asked catcher Gary Sanchez, also Judge's longtime minor-league teammate. "I've seen him hit home runs before, but that one was just incredible." As Judge high-fived teammates in the dugout, the crowd of 46,438 showered him with chants of "MVP!" which had become a common musical refrain among the bleacher creatures. With a swing like that, suddenly, it was not so crazy to think that if anybody could hit a ball out of Yankee Stadium, it was this rookie wonder.

There is power and precision to his swing. But it's not just the style in which he was bashing the baseball, shattering TV screens, and setting rookie records. Judge was running roughshod over the American League. On top of that, his number 99 jersey had become baseball's hottest selling item. But for all of the success, none of it appeared to be changing who he is. Judge knows his place. He makes sure to arrive early enough to use the batting cage before the rush of established players, stays out of the training room during the veterans' preferred times, and generally keeps his mouth shut. Should his attitude ever exceed his standing, though, Judge can count on left fielder Brett Gardner to keep his size-17 feet planted firmly on the ground.

Gardner needles teammates and clubhouse guys alike, but he takes special pleasure in going after Judge. One minute he's snatched a bag of sunflower seeds from the rookie's big hands and thrown it onto the field, and the next he's threatened to prank his friend and record it on hidden camera. "He started it!" Gardner insisted. "The other day he dumped a bucket of cold water on me in the shower. Unprovoked!" Judge sat by at his locker with a smile of satisfaction, like the new kid at school who finally felt accepted by the established kids.

COSTLY JERSEY

As of July 15, 2017, Aaron Judge led the major leagues in jersey sales, and according to MLB, Judge had the most popular batting practice jersey of any All-Star Game in the last decade. The jersey he wore during his major-league debut was sold at auction that July, for $157,000. The price paid made Judge's jersey the costliest from any of North America's four major sports in the past 15 years, with Stephen Curry's jersey from the 2017 NBA Finals previously the most expensive at $135,000.

Memorabilia centered on Judge proved to be particularly popular among buyers and collectors. In July, a rookie card the 25-year-old signed was sold on eBay for more than $14,000, while the jersey he wore when hitting his first career grand slam was purchased for $45,000.

Summer Sizzle

Since his major-league debut in 2016, Judge had been named an All-Star in 2017 with the most votes of any American League player, won that year's Home Run Derby, and broke the New York Yankees' rookie record for most home runs in a season (beating Joe DiMaggio's 29 before the All-Star break). He was voted the American League's Player of the Month for June, as well as American League Rookie of the Month for the third consecutive time.

He claimed his first league Player of the Month award in a noteworthy fashion: .324 batting average, 10 home runs, 25 runs batted in, 30 runs scored, five doubles, a triple, and two stolen bases. He was the first American League player to earn three Rookie of the Month awards in a single season since José Abreu of the Chicago White Sox in 2014 and the first American Leaguer to garner three consecutive Rookie of the Month awards since Mike Trout of the Los Angeles Angels of Anaheim took home the honor in four consecutive months in 2012 (May–August).

Among qualified American League batters, the 25-year-old Judge finished the month of June ranked first in runs scored, walks, and on-base percentage; second in batting average, home runs, and triples; third in slugging percentage; and tied for fifth in runs batted in. During one particularly torrid three-game stretch against the Baltimore Orioles, from June 10 to 12, he batted 9-for-12 with four home runs, eight runs batted in, 10 runs scored, and two doubles. Included in his offensive outbreak was a 4-for-4 effort on June 11, which included his third multi-homer game of the season. Judge finished the month of June pacing the American League in two of the three Triple Crown categories. He led the league in home runs (30) and runs batted in (62), and Judge (.326) trailed only Houston's José Altuve (.330) for the highest batting average.

"He is putting on the most amazing display I think I have ever seen," claimed John Sterling, who has witnessed five World Series championships in his 28 years calling Yankees games. That's not bad for a kid who batted .179 in 27 games with New York in 2016 and wasn't assured a spot on the major-league Opening Day roster until the end of spring training, in March 2017. "Words can't describe how proud of him we are," said Judge's father, Wayne. "If [success] happens to end tomorrow, he's the type of kid who will say, 'It was meant to be,' and move on."

THE BAMBINO

Babe Ruth was baseball's first great home-run hitter, and fans flocked to see him play. He changed the game of baseball.

Ruth joined the Boston Red Sox in 1914 and quickly became one of the best pitchers in the major leagues. He also turned out to be a powerful hitter. In 1918, the Red Sox made Babe an outfielder on the days he did not pitch. He led the league in home runs with 11. In 1920, he was traded to the New York Yankees and switched permanently to the outfield so he could concentrate on hitting.

In 1920, Ruth hit 54 home runs. No one had hit more than 29 in a season before (Babe himself had done that in 1919). From 1926 to 1931, he averaged more than 50 home runs a year. He hit 60 home runs in 1927 and 714 home runs in his career, both records that stood for a long time. (Roger Maris hit 61 home runs for the Yankees in 1961, and Hank Aaron hit his 715th home run in 1974. Both those records have since been surpassed.)

In all, Babe led the American League in home runs 12 times and in RBIs six times. "The Sultan of Swat" led the Yankees to seven World Series. Yankee Stadium was built to hold the crowds that came to see him. It was known as "The House That Ruth Built." He retired in 1935, and in 1936 he became one of the first players selected to the National Baseball Hall of Fame.

Fan Favorite

It isn't difficult to figure out who is the most popular player on the Yankees' roster these days. At Yankee Stadium it is hard to walk 10 feet through a corridor and not encounter someone wearing a number 99 T-shirt or number 99 Judge jersey. Employees of the Yankees team stores scramble to keep his replica jerseys in stock. In less than four months time, New York had already adopted Judge as its favorite son.

During the game the crowd roars in delight when the public address announcer bellows, "All rise for number 99, Judge." The Yankee Stadium video scoreboard now displays a gavel graphic and the words ALL RISE before Judge's first at-bat of each game. At this point, fans might as well remain standing until he's done. And they always wait until Judge has finished batting before heading to the restrooms. "We don't want to miss Judge!" they exclaim. The Judge effect was seen on television screens, too, as the team's YES Network reported ratings up 57 percent year over year.

Judge's sudden popularity stemmed from his willingness to sign autographs and interact with fans and also the fact that he is a home-grown Yankee rather than an established player acquired from else-where. In that respect, Judge is in the tradition of an earlier fan favorite, Derek Jeter, whose number 2 jersey seemed to be everywhere at the Stadium when he was playing. Now there has been a clear shift toward number 99.

His aura was playing outside of the Bronx too. Nearly every media outlet from *People* to TMZ, Jimmy Kimmel to *Good Morning America*, not to mention the daily sports newspapers, were lined up hoping to interview the New York Yankees rookie player. Yet it appeared all the attention was not going to his head or swelling his ego. He carried himself in the way all the greats do, with that certain level of confidence and poise.

He truly did it all on a baseball diamond. He mashed ridiculous homers and made young fans' dreams come true. Broadcasters gushed that his bombs were Ruthian. And his attitude toward fans recalls Joe DiMaggio's famous line: "There is always some kid who may be seeing me for the first or last time. I owe him my best." The list goes on and on and on. He had another exploit of awesomeness on July 21, as the Yankees were protecting a slim 4–1 lead over the Seattle Mariners at Safeco Field.

The ninth inning is usually the tensest time in a ballgame. But the anxious moment never throws Judge off his game. Just before the bottom of the ninth inning began, he passed the time by playing a casual game of catch with a young Mariners fan in the right field stands. Judge said after the game that it was just a spur of the moment thing. "I had some extra time, and I saw a kid with a glove and threw him a few balls." That'll definitely be a moment the lucky fan will remember for a long, long time.

Making a fan's day is nothing new for him. At the start of an inning, after he's taken his warmup throws, Judge always jogs over to the outfield wall and plops a baseball in a youngster's outstretched glove. The kid receiving the gift from one of the biggest young stars of the game always goes bonkers with happiness.

CHAPTER 12

DIFFERENCE MAKER

THE VERDICT IS in: the Yankees are officially marketing Judge as the star attraction in the Bronx after the rookie's hot start to the season. In May, the Yankees unveiled "The Judge's Chambers," a specific cheering section for their towering outfielder in the right field stands directly behind the real estate where Judge plays. This cheering section draws huge crowds of fans who show up in long white cotton wigs and wearing black judges' robes emblazoned with the Yankees logo.

The three-row, 18-seat area near Section 104 in the lower level in right field features faux wood paneling around the front and back rows to resemble a courtroom's jury box, plus "THE JUDGE'S CHAM-BERS" clearly written in capital letters along the back of the paneling. It also includes some judge's props, like foam gavels, for anyone sitting in the section.

There's a catch: you can't buy tickets to sit there. Instead, the team will choose specific fans and their families to sit in the seats. "It's pretty cool," said Judge of the new seating area. "When you come to a game, it's supposed to be fun for the players and fans. I feel like it might be something that's fun for the fans out there."

He didn't know about it beforehand. "They just brought it up to me and said, 'Hey, this is what we're going to do.' I think it turned out great." Judge was surprised to already have a permanent spot in the stadium: "It's pretty unreal. I never would have thought so soon. But the fans like it, so I'm glad they're having fun."

For a player whose mounting popularity enabled him to receive more All-Star votes than any American Leaguer, who graced the cover of *Sports Illustrated*, and who earlier in the season manager Joe Girardi likened to Derek Jeter in the way he handles himself, the creation of "The Judge's Chambers" section is the latest form of praise heaped on the 25-year-old outfielder. Hall of Famers Babe Ruth and Reggie Jackson patrolled right field for the Bombers, and although Mr. October had a candy bar that bore his name, neither the Bambino nor Jackson ever had an entire seating section named after them. That's pretty good for someone who hasn't even played a full season in the majors.

THE REGGIE! BAR

Reggie Jackson famously boasted that if he ever played in New York, they'd name a candy bar after him. Sure enough, after his memorable performance in the 1977 World Series, he got his wish. Manufactured by Standard Brands Confectionary, the Reggie! candy bar was a round, 25-cent patty of chocolate-covered caramel and peanuts. Cracked teammate Catfish Hunter: "When you unwrap a Reggie! bar, it tells you how good it is."

Prior to the 1978 Yankees home opener, Standard Brands handed out free Reggie! bars as a sales promotion gimmick to the

44,667 fans who passed through the turnstiles. In the game's first inning, Jackson, who had homered on his last three swings of the 1977 World Series at Yankee Stadium, connected again on his first cut of the home season, smashing a three-run homer off Chicago's Wilbur Wood in the Yankees' 4–2 win over the White Sox.

When Jackson took his position in right field to start the second inning, the fans threw thousands of Reggie! bars onto the field in tribute. The game was delayed about five minutes for groundskeepers to gather the candy.

Game Changer

Judge's batting practices had become must-see shows for fans, teammates, and opposing players, drawing oohs and aahs whenever he sent a long, majestic drive far into the stands. But his game is not based on sheer size and strength alone, as he showed when he sprinted into the right-center field gap to make a diving, backhanded catch on the warning track that preserved the Yankees' 3–2 victory over the Tampa Bay Rays at Tropicana Field, on May 21. It was the key play in a much-needed victory for the Yankees, ending a three-game losing streak, and propelling them into first place in the American League East division.

"Not much you can do other than tip your cap," said Evan Longoria, who hit the ball Judge caught. "It was a great play, and it ended up saving the game for them. We'll be watching it on *SportsCenter* for a while."

There may be catches that are as good, but it is hard to imagine one surpassing it. With a man on base, he took a great route to the ball and in an all-out sprint, launched his body horizontally and plucked the sphere out of the air a few inches off the turf. And he held onto the ball as he hit the ground with a thud after landing at the edge of the warning track, robbing the batter of an extra-base hit and protecting a one-run lead. There was more. He skidded on his stomach and, from his knees, threw the ball back toward the infield. As the icing on the cake, his effort resulted in a double play.

The Yankees' dugout erupted as it would on one of his 450-foot home runs. But Judge was nonchalant after the play and resumed his position without even a smile. But when he returned to the dugout at the end of the sixth inning, he was greeted by high-fives and attaboys and appreciation from his teammates. "It saved the game for us," said Yankees manager Girardi.

The play showed not just Judge's raw athleticism, but also showed that even on a day when he struck out four times, he could find ways to influence a game. "I wasn't doing it on offense so I had to do something on defense to help the team," he said. "That's what I'm getting paid to do out there, make plays." Judge's breakout season wasn't limited to a series of monster home runs. His offensive production wowed people, but he impressed people with his defense, as well.

I had to do something to help the team."
—Aaron Judge

Ballpark Buster

Judge can do things nobody else can. During the Home Run Derby, he hit a batted ball that struck the roof of Miami's Marlins Park, and on July 21, he clubbed a colossal three-run homer so far that it broke Statcast. The big slugger clobbered a hanging curveball from Seattle's Andrew Moore into the second deck in left field, with the ball landing three rows from the top of the stadium. No one has hit one out of

Safeco Field during a game since the ballpark opened midway through the 1999 season. His 31st home run in the fifth inning, and first since that immense power display at the Home Run Derby, was memorable and nearly historic. At that point in the season nearly half his home runs (15) had been hit at least 425 feet and this one—measured at 440—gave two new teammates a chance to witness his power firsthand.

Players in the bullpen were craning their necks to try to get a look at where the ball landed. Relief pitcher David Robertson, acquired from the Chicago White Sox a week earlier, said that it looked like Judge was playing in a bandbox. "It's not fair. It's like he is playing on a Little League field," he said. "I have never seen anyone hit a home run like that."

Third baseman Todd Frazier, who came over in the same trade, was slack-jawed as he sat in the dugout when Judge hit his home run. "It's like one of the Seven Wonders of the World," said Frazier. "It's something to see. You just don't see balls hit that far and that high. It's not only that far, it's how high they go and with such ease and no effort. It's just A to B and *pow*. It's a really beautiful thing." According to Girardi, hitting coach Alan Cockrell, a former Mariners hitting coach, told him, "That's the farthest ball he has seen hit here."

No player has ever hit a ball out of Safeco Field in a game—though the Mariners' Nelson Cruz did in batting practice in 2016—and it is hard to imagine many coming as close as Judge did. Though the home run was estimated at 440 feet, its true distance was hard to determine. Statcast, the analytics tool that uses high-speed, pitch-tracking cameras to gather data on each pitch, did not register a distance on the home run, because it soared too high into the stratosphere to be tracked.

"I thought it was going out of the stadium," said teammate Clint Frazier. "You think people would get bored seeing him hit a ball that far, but he surprises everybody every time he goes out there and hits a ball in a spot where no one else can."

As usual, the person who appeared to be the least impressed with Judge's tape-measure home run was Judge. He put his head down as soon as he connected and ran around the bases as if he was in a hurry to get back to the dugout—and he was the first one back in, beating two teammates, the two baserunners who were waiting to greet him at home plate.

Amazing Creature

Judge's superhuman display of brute strength meeting hand-eye coordination was the game's decisive shot. In all, he drove in four runs in the Yankees' 5–1 victory over the Mariners; he put them ahead with a sacrifice fly to deep center field before adding the jaw-dropping three-run homer. It was the type of performance that he and the team really needed. Boosting their record to 50-45, it was the Yankees' second straight win, something they had done just once since June 11-12.

In short order, Judge had become one of baseball's biggest stars, largely because he hit some of baseball's most dramatic home runs. But special players find ways to help their team even when they're not hitting at their best. Judge can do more than just slam home runs with his bat, as he showcased his cannon of an arm in a game against the Minnesota Twins, on July 17. With the bases loaded and no outs, Twins third baseman Miguel Sanó lashed a rocket to right field that Judge effortlessly caught. Tagging from third base, Brian Dozier was gunned down by Judge's perfect one-hop throw to complete the double play. Judge's throw home was unleashed at nearly 98 miles per hour and from 262 feet away. "That's it?" Judge joked. "I've got to get something more behind that."

It was the hardest throw on an assist for Judge in his career and marked his fourth assist of the season. Yankees catcher Austin Romine caught the ball on a bounce and seamlessly tagged Dozier, who tried to slip his left hand across home plate. Judge said that he practices similar plays each day during batting practice when the Yankees' outfielders throw to bases.

With terrific range and a strong, accurate throwing arm, Judge has made several eye-popping plays, proving his value as a defender. Even when the hits don't come, he has the ability to range far to make highlight-reel catches. He is so big and so athletic, given his body length and vertical jumping ability, it is likely that fans will for many years be watching video of him pulling back would-be home runs that few other outfielders in history could have reached.

Nothing would make the "Bleacher Creatures" happier. The Bleacher Creatures are a fanatical group of diehard Yankees rooters who are known for their imaginative "Roll Call" that starts each game, in which the Creatures chant the name of each starting position player—"*Aa*-ron *Ju*-dge! *Aa*-ron *Ju*-dge!" clap-clap-clapclapclap—until each one responds with a wave, a tip of the hat or something more inventive. The Bleacher Creatures occupy section 203 in the right field bleachers of Yankee Stadium, located right behind where Judge presides.

ROLL CALL

The Roll Call tradition started in the early 1990s and has been one of the trademarks of Yankee Stadium ever since. The Bleacher Creatures' roll call occurs in the top of the first inning, when the Yankees are on the field, right after the starting pitcher throws the game's first pitch. The Creatures move through the defensive alignment, going from the center fielder to the left fielder, right fielder, first baseman, second baseman, shortstop and third baseman, in that order.

Everyone in the section stands and begins clapping their hands. The group then chants the player's name until there is a response, usually a perfunctory wave of the glove. Some Yankees, however, respond with extra enthusiasm, such as left fielder Brett Gardner, who typically flexes his muscles in what is called his "gun show," and right fielder Aaron Judge, who turns to face the Creatures, points to them, and taps his glove two times.

CHAPTER 13

DEALING WITH ADVERSITY

EVER SINCE WINNING the Home Run Derby on July 11, Aaron Judge had been in a funk at the plate. After four games in Boston he managed just one infield single in 18 at-bats against the Red Sox, though Jackie Bradley Jr. dramatically stole a two-run homer from him in the finale. Judge wasn't much better in a 4–2 Yankees loss the next night in Minnesota's Target Field, going 0-for-3 with an intentional walk, that extended Judge's slump to 1-for-21.

The smile and the confident walk were still there. He walked into the Yankees clubhouse with no visible sign of anxiety, even though he had managed only one infield single in 21 at-bats since the All-Star break—the first rough stretch of his remarkably dominant season. Why stress? He was still leading the major leagues with 30 home runs, and he ranked among the American League leaders in most offensive categories. And this slump, after all, was nothing like what he went through in August and September of 2016, when he batted .179 in his first 27 games as a Yankee.

"Everything's going to work out," he said flashing that ready grin. "It's baseball. This is a crazy game we play. You're going to have those times you can't get out, and those times where you can do everything right and the ball does not fall."

Fickle Game

At the mention of a residual fatigue factor possibly being at play following his impressive Home Run Derby win from the week before, Judge smiled and said: "I didn't look fatigued in the Derby, did I? I feel I had four days off. [I'm] fresh and ready to go." That statement was hard to argue with when Judge and the Yankees broke out of their respective hitting slumps with a 6–3 victory over the Minnesota Twins, on July 18. Judge, mired in a 1-for-22 free fall, went 2-for-4 with a run batted in, singling in the go-ahead run in the fifth inning. The Yankees hadn't scored more than four runs in a game since the All-Star break and hadn't pushed across six runs since July 5, a 7–6 loss to the Toronto Blue Jays at Yankee Stadium.

Judge's slump certainly did not help during that difficult stretch. In a season in which he had so much success and so few struggles, even a five-game stretch without a multi-hit game or a gargantuan homer raised eyebrows. Judge talked about his downturn with more bemusement than concern. "I've had stretches like this even this year," he said. He noted an 0-for-4 with four strikeouts on May 21 against Tampa Bay, followed by an 0-for-3 the next day against Kansas City at Yankee Stadium. Judge then went 4-for-9 in the next three games.

"It's just trusting the process that got me where I am," he said. "If I start making little changes here and there, it may be a quick fix, but in the long haul it won't help me out."

None of Judge's teammates seemed overly concerned. "He set a really high standard for himself, and for other people," said teammate Matt Holliday. "He's fine with it. He's handled it really well, and he's a very mature kid. I don't think it's a problem at all."

It won't be. "Baseball's fickle, man," third baseman Chase Headley added. "When things go your way, they can snowball. When they don't go your way, they can snowball."

After winning the Home Run Derby, Judge went 31 at-bats without a home run. His average dropped 18 points in a week, which might have caused a less grounded player to doubt himself. But as young as Judge is, only 25, he's been blessed with quiet swagger and a limitless reservoir of self-confidence. He showed no outward sign of losing his mojo.

66

It's baseball. This is a crazy game we play."

—Aaron Judge

"It's a Tough League"

The Yankees limped into Seattle's Safeco Field to begin a four-game series against the Mariners, on July 20. New York had dropped to third place, treading water with a 48-45 record, four and a half games behind the Boston Red Sox. The Yankees' offense was stalling out. Hitters rarely put together quality at-bats, situational hitting was abysmal, and numerous baserunners were left stranded because a clutch two-out hit was a rarity. Judge was in a 4-for-30 slump. The Yankees were in dire need of greater production for their right-handed slugger. With a .167 batting average and 38 strikeouts in 84 at-bats to start out the second half of the season, Judge looked alternately exhausted and overwhelmed.

It was reasonable to expect he wouldn't maintain those Triple Crown–like numbers from the first half, but Yankees fans were dismayed at how quickly the 25-year-old rookie had seemed to regress. According to scouts, pitchers had adjusted to Judge by challenging him with fastballs around the eyes and sliders just off the outside corner. Manager Joe Girardi was quick to defend Judge, reminding reporters that hitting slumps are contagious and that Judge hadn't been alone in his struggles. Still, Judge acknowledged that he had let down his team by putting himself in too many two-strike positions. "I'm just not executing when I get my pitch to hit," he said. "When you miss your pitch to hit in the big leagues, bad things can happen."

While many observers believed Judge's problems could be traced to the mechanics of his swing, the hitting coach Alan Cockrell believed they were more related to Judge's lack of adjustment to how pitchers have changed their plans of attack since the break. Cockrell hinted that the sequencing of pitches used against Judge was different. Mostly, though, he said Judge was pressing. "You end up trying to do a little more, a little extra," he said. "He wants to win. He wants to contribute. He's a very determined, very hard-working kid. But it's a hard season and a tough league. You can't try to do extra."

Many veterans taper their training later in the season, but Judge said he had not altered his routine. He stills lifts weights and does core exercises for about 30 minutes after games, and he has not switched to a lighter bat, as experienced players sometimes do later in the season. Some players cut back on batting practice, but Judge took early extra sessions. He said that he did not feel worn down. "If I don't work out, I feel like I get weak," he said. "If I'm working out every day, I feel like I put my body in the best position to go out there and play every day."

SUPERSTITIOUS STAR

During the slump, Aaron Judge divulged a habit he uses during at-bats when he feels the need to refocus and slow things down. And it's often so subtle that even his New York Yankees teammates have scarcely noticed. It involves reaching down and picking up some dirt in between pitches. "It's just a way of slowing things down, taking an extra two or three seconds to grab some dirt," said Judge, who has used the dirt-scooping practice since his college days at Fresno State, after he read a book co-written by sports psychologists Ken Ravizza and Tom Hanson entitled *Heads-Up Baseball: Playing the Game One Pitch at a Time*.

"For me, all my negative thoughts that I have about, 'How did you miss that pitch? Why did you miss that pitch? You shouldn't have missed that pitch.' I kind of crush it up, and once I'm done doing that, I just toss it aside. Basically tossing all those thoughts out, like, 'Hey, that's done with. That's over with now. Start fresh and get back in the box and get back to your positive thoughts and get back to your approach.'"

Judge admits he has another weird habit during games. It begins moments before first pitch—with a superstition. He pops two pieces of Dubble Bubble sugar-free bubblegum in his mouth. Until he makes an out, he'll continue to chew it. If he picks up a hit in his first at-bat, the gum stays in. Another hit, and he keeps chewing. "Hopefully, by the end of the night, I have a nasty, old, unflavored piece of gum in my mouth," he said.

The tradition started in college, and he doesn't plan on changing it. His outs do have a sweet ending, because if he makes one, he throws away the old gum and takes two fresh pieces. If he goes 3-for-3 and the game takes four hours to play, Judge will just keep gnawing on the old gum, with no thought of changing it out or adding a new piece. "No, I keep it in there," he says. "It is lucky." Occasionally, Judge will switch it up if he's in a rut. He'll go with sunflower seeds, available next to the gum in the middle of the Bombers' dugout.

Grin and Bear It

Adding insult to injury, baseball's most famous gap-toothed smile needed a little unexpected dental work. After Brett Gardner hit a game-winning home run in the Yankees' 6–5, 11-inning win over the Tampa Bay Rays on July 27, Judge jumped into a wild postgame celebration that proved costly when Gardner's helmet hit him in the mouth, knocking out half of his front left tooth. Judge said he wanted to pick up Gardner's loose helmet, which had been tossed to the ground after crossing home plate, so that one of his teammates wouldn't step on it and be accidentally injured. "I didn't want anybody breaking an ankle," he said.

But the slugging right fielder was the one who ended up getting hurt. A teammate jumped just as Judge, behind him, bent his head forward, and the helmet hit him in the mouth. "It got me pretty good," he said. Much to Judge's chagrin, the incident was captured on video and spread quickly on social media. His teammates weren't going to let him forget the mishap anytime soon. "I'm sure the ribbing from his teammates will continue for a few days," said Girardi. "This will not stop after today."

After a visit to the dentist the next morning, Judge showed up for the game that night with his smile newly restored by a temporary cap on the tooth. "It's fixed now, and we're good to go," he said.

The chipped tooth was Judge's latest hardship since the All-Star break, after which little had gone right for him. Since the Home Run Derby, he had batted .180, with just three home runs and nine hits in

50 at-bats. Over the 14 games since the All-Star Game, Judge's batting average dropped by 18 points, to .308, and his slugging percentage had plummeted by 40 points, to .644. He still led the American League with 33 homers and was second with 74 runs batted in. Judge accepted the dental misadventure with customary good humor. "Next time I pick up a helmet," he said, "I'm tossing it."

Two days later, the Yankees beat the Rays, 5–4, on Gardner's game-winning single in the ninth inning. This time, Judge exercised a bit more caution during the team's celebration. Remembering the dental damage from a similar revelry, Judge covered his mouth, used his hand as a makeshift mouth guard, and finally entered the sea of high-fives and Gatorade showers to congratulate Gardner on his second game-ending hit in three days while avoiding personal harm.

Even though the homers were no longer flying at an incredible pace, Judge was still getting on base, working deep into counts, and getting his share of base on balls. Ultimately, Judge was walked 127 times in the 2017 regular season, the most of any American League batter and a Major League Baseball rookie record. So there's something to be said for the fear factor, which Judge patented like no one else in the Yankees lineup.

Fans eagerly anticipated the game when Judge would finally bust out of his slump and put the Baby Bombers onto his broad shoulders and carry them to the pennant. When the Yankees beat the Toronto Blue Jays in an 11–5 blowout, on August 9, however, there was still no sign of Judge, who had another hitless game and saw his average drop to .294, down 35 points since the All-Star break.

Strikeout Record

Records are made to be broken, but some records nobody wants to break. Judge broke one of those marks, setting an MLB record of dubious distinction. He struck out in 37 games in a row. He began his whiff streak on July 8. Along the way he passed Cincinnati's Adam Dunn, the "Big Donkey," who struck out in 32 games in a row, the most of any position player. Then he surpassed the record for a pitcher, 35 games in a row, set by Bill Stoneman of the Montreal Expos, in 1971.

His statistics took a massive nosedive in nearly every category during the strikeout streak. Judge had dropped his batting average by 40 points since the Home Run Derby, including 41 strikeouts in 89 at-bats. It's remarkable how closely he resembled the late 2016 version of himself. Judge was whiffing about 32 percent of the time he stepped to the plate. His manager, Girardi, continued to issue one vote of confidence after another, although he admitted benching Judge, even for a day or two, was on the table. "It's something I can think about. I'm trying to get him back on track," said the manager. "It's been a struggle in the second half."

While Judge struggled it was catcher Gary Sanchez who picked up the slack. Sanchez blasted two home runs at Comerica Park, on August 22, one a mammoth shot estimated at 493 feet. But Judge's polite swagger also resonated. "I think I've still got him by two feet," said Judge with a grin, still the reigning 2017 home-run distance leader.

Though he shrugged it aside, Judge's record streak of 37 games with at least one strikeout ended during the Yankees' 13–4 pounding of the Detroit Tigers. The struggling Judge was bumped one spot down the order—swapping places with the scorching Sanchez, now with 11 home runs over his last 24 games, dating to July 27. As the cleanup hitter, Judge walked his first three times up and singled in a run before being subbed out by a pinch-hitter in the seventh inning, with the Yankees ahead 11–1. "Not really," he said of feeling any relief, ending a strikeout streak that was the longest by any big-league position player. "Like I said, I don't even think about it. I only think about it when [the media] ask me."

Judge's slump was now in its sixth week. Since the All-Star break, the Yankees had gotten just nine extra-base hits out of him, and his batting average had plummeted nearly 50 points, from .329 to .282. He said he did not feel worn down by a long season or frustrated by the multitude of strikeouts. "There's nothing I can really do. It happens," said

Judge. "I'm going to strike out." Historically, baseball's most powerful hitters do strike out in bunches. But for the greatest of the greats, it's what they do *between* the strikeouts that really matter.

STRIKE THREE, YER OUT!

In today's game of baseball, as strikeout rates increase and become more accepted, strikeouts in and of themselves are becoming less and less an effective way to sort good hitters from bad. History indicates that many batters who frequently whiff are extremely productive hitters. To identify the best hitters, today's sabermetricians look at how many outs a batter makes, not how the batter makes outs. The analysts look at how much damage a batter does rather than focusing on his strikeouts.

Babe Ruth (1,330) held the all-time record for career strikeouts for 35 years. Then Mickey Mantle (1,710) passed him and held the record for 14 years. Willie Stargell (1,936) passed him and held the record for four years. Reggie Jackson (2,597) then stole the record and has held it for 34 years. All four players are immortal Hall of Famers. So how bad can strikeouts really be when some of the best hitters ever to play the game struck out the most?

CHAPTER 14
THE FACE OF THE GAME

THE FACES OF baseball have often been players from the New York Yankees, such as Babe Ruth, Lou Gehrig, Joe DiMaggio, Mickey Mantle, and Derek Jeter. Aaron Judge has the potential to be next in line, and he has the demeanor too. He seemingly never takes credit when the Yankees win; instead he defers all praise to his teammates.

Judge is quickly emerging as the future of not only the Yankees, but also the heir apparent to Jeter as baseball's next superstar that truly transcends the sport. Count the baseball commissioner Rob Manfred as one of Judge's biggest fans. He called Judge, "absolutely phenomenal. There is no other word to describe it. He is a tremendous talent on the field and really appealing off the field." Manfred was not shy about his expectations for Judge, saying he is the type of player "who can become the face of the game."

Major League Baseball and the comedy video website *Funny or Die* teamed up to celebrate the popular New York outfielder with a Judge-Con promotion in which four actors and comics were enlisted to dress as judges and make appearances throughout New York City, including a ride on the subway and stops at Yankee Stadium and Rockefeller Center.

The agent David Matranga of PSI Sports Management, which represents Judge, said the 25-year-old has kept his mind on pitchers, not corporate pitches. "We've had quite a few offers from various markets and brands. It just keeps coming every day," said the agent. "He's got a lot of people pulling at him, but right now Aaron just wants to keep his focus on the Yankees."

Role Model

Judge doesn't just sit atop the rankings of baseball's best home run hitters—he literally towers above his competition. Just ask former Red Sox slugger David Ortiz. "Look at Judge," said Big Papi. "Look at him. That's scary, man. That's the scariest thing I've ever seen." Like all exceptional athletes, Judge leaves fans certain they could not possibly do what he does. He makes adults feel in awe, even the ones he plays against. "It's just that he's so big," said Red Sox outfielder Mookie Betts. "For a human to get like that is pretty amazing to me."

Yes, Judge is a physical revelation. He is the biggest, the strongest, and hits the ball the hardest. But he doesn't flip his bat into the air. He puts his head down and jogs around the bases. He's all business. He is the modern epitome of what a traditional baseball star can be. His peers frequently cite him as a model of good sportsmanship and virtue.

"The kid seems to have his head on his shoulders the right way," said former Yankees catcher John Flaherty, now a broadcaster for the team. "He seems to say the right thing. It's about team first, it's not about him." Washington Nationals pitcher Stephen Strasburg agreed: "Judge has a good head on his shoulders and he plays the game the right way."

Tampa Bay's ace pitcher Chris Archer is also on the Judge bandwagon: "You can tell he's very humble and keeps his nose clean."

Partly because of the busy schedule—162 games in 183 days—baseball players don't have much time for marketing during the season. And when it comes to page views, clicks, and tweets, baseball players lag behind the NFL and NBA players who have connected far better with younger audiences. Alex Rodriguez, the former Yankees infielder with 696 career home runs, raved about Judge's physical attributes and how his success could impact the future of the sport.

"For the first time in a long time, we have a LeBron James type of personality and size that can transcend sports," said Rodriguez. "Here's a guy who is 6-foot-7, 275 pounds, 9 percent body fat, 32-inch vertical [leap]. The guy bench presses 400 pounds, squats 500 pounds, and he's an amazing figure. For the next generation to say, 'Well, there's a guy who can be a tight end and an All-Pro, and he chose baseball. Why can't I?' So hopefully kids are taking notes on Aaron Judge."

Late Night Stunt

During the early summer of 2017, Judge was already the talk of baseball, the Yankees' breakout star, and one of the biggest athletes in New York—literally and figuratively. Yet many of his fans wouldn't even recognize him if they were in a face-to-face conversation. That was evident after watching the skit Judge did for Jimmy Fallon on *The Tonight Show*. The gag involved him posing as an interviewer asking fans: "What do you think about Aaron Judge?"

Doing his best Clark Kent impression, Judge sat behind a desk in New York's Bryant Park to conceal his 6-foot-7 frame. The majors' home-run leader's only disguise was a pair of hip black-rimmed eyeglasses and a blue sportcoat—and he managed to fool about a half dozen fans as they chatted next to him.

"When I was going through it, I didn't think I was doing well at all. They did a lot of editing," he said. "There were quite a few moments where it was a little awkward silence."

Judge said he interviewed about 20 fans. Some fans recognized him right away. Those interviews didn't make the cut, but one male fan wearing a Yankees cap said he felt "Adam" Judge would be a superstar. "People say I kind of look like him," Judge told the fan while holding a photograph of himself wearing a Yankees uniform.

"A little bit," the fan said.

Another memorable exchange occurred when the right fielder held up the cover of *Sports Illustrated*, which featured Judge on the cover. "I had a feeling, man," the fan who initially did not recognize him said before mentioning a certain characteristic of Judge's front teeth. "The gap, it was the gap. There's only two gaps in New York—you and [former New York Giants football star Michael] Strahan, man."

Overall, Judge felt the routine went over better than he thought. "I've been getting texts and calls all day about it," said Judge. "I'm just glad people enjoyed it."

Living for the City

By the 2017 All-Star Game, New York Yankees outfielder Judge was no longer completely anonymous. A monstrous rookie season had rocketed him into the national spotlight. Yet he was still the same modest young man he'd always been. On the field he was an All-Star, but off the field he was living out of two suitcases in an art deco hotel in Times Square. At the time of his *Sports Illustrated* cover shoot, he said he was wary of renting an apartment lest he be sent back to Scranton. "I don't want to put all my cards that I'm going to be in New York and then I go to Triple-A. Maybe next year, if everything goes well."

Just as New York had adopted Judge as its favorite son, he had embraced the city in an equally accepting way. He delighted in the hotel elevator rides to and from the lobby, where he interacted with guests from all over the world, most of whom had no idea who he was. For a young man who grew up in a place where he often went a week or two without seeing an unfamiliar face, he seemed to have made a seamless transition to the big city.

❝

It's definitely different from what I knew back home, but I love the city."

—Aaron Judge

He walked among the late-night tourists in midtown Manhattan after games. The international tourists might not recognize him—yet—but most everyone else in the neighborhood certainly does by now. "Look, it's him," is a familiar whisper Judge hears more and more these days. This place could not be less like Linden, where one could go weeks without seeing a stranger. But the Yankees slugger does not hide behind a security detail. He doesn't hide, period.

His favorite Times Square activity is getting frozen yogurt at midnight. "It's exciting," he said. "Here you can get any food you want at any hour. It's definitely different from what I knew back home, but I love the city."

He's even started to play the piano again, something he used to mess around with at his grandmother's house as a kid.

BEING FAMOUS

How has his life changed for Aaron Judge now that everyone recognizes him? Not that much. He has always been easily recognized. At Fresno State he was a star outfielder who drew stares every time he entered a room. There is nowhere for a 6-foot-7, 282-pound man to hide. He is used to the feeling of eyes on him.

Perhaps the biggest difference is how often people approach him now, though he always got some of that attention. "You're huge!" passersby would say. "What do you play?" He'd grin and answer, "Fantasy football."

Today the questions tend to be requests, usually for photos. He tries to agree to them all. "That could be the only time they meet me," he said. "I don't want to leave the impression that I didn't have the five seconds to say hello." When they see him, fans like to inform him, "You're Aaron Judge!" He doesn't need to introduce himself to opposing teams, either. The Yankees' right fielder and biggest Baby Bomber was off to the most powerful start to a season ever by a rookie.

Back on Track

Twenty years has passed since Major League Baseball instituted inter-league play, and the average fan can't get enough of it. For one week every summer, the excitement level in the city of New York reaches a fever pitch during the annual Subway Series between the Mets and Yankees. The four-game series, split between the Bronx and Queens, brings great passion from fans both in support of their team and against the other.

Playing in his first game at Citi Field, on August 20, the Yankees' 25-year-old rookie slugger led off the fourth inning of the Yankees' 5–3 win by demolishing a hanging slider from Mets starter Robert Gsellman that landed in the third deck of left field at Citi Field and then one-hopped into Section 536—an area where fans should never expect to receive home-run balls. "Home runs like that, you just have to watch them," said Gsellman.

The home run was measured at 457 feet, but Judge's teammates thought it went farther. "I've never seen a ball go up there," said Chase Headley. "I don't know how many balls have gone up there, but if that only went [457 feet], then no ball is going over 500 feet because that ball was crushed." Didi Gregorius provided his own estimate: "530 feet, that's what I've been telling everybody." Added Joe Girardi: "I mean, I think we all kind of say, 'Wow.' You just don't see that every day."

Judge, who hit four balls 500-plus feet en route to his title at the Home Run Derby, simply put his head down the minute he connected and started to trot around the bases. "They all feel the same," said the always-modest Judge. "Usually when you get it on the sweet spot of the bat you don't really feel it." Even though he paid little attention as he ran around the bases, Judge's teammates helped him out. "They pointed to where it went," he said.

Judge owned the five hardest-hit balls in the majors through August 20th: 121 miles per hour, 119, 118.6, 118.4, and the one against the Mets, 117. He had eight hits that traveled at least 115 mph. The rest of baseball had 13. Judge was the American League home-run leader with 37, including two in his last three games. The game against the Mets marked his second multi-hit game of the second half and first since July 18. The power surge was an encouraging sign that he'd finally found his swing again.

First-Year Marvel

It has been a marvelous rookie season for Judge. He started out like a supernova that would replace Mike Trout and Bryce Harper as the Next Great Thing. It wasn't just the Yankees who flourished under Judge—the industry itself fell in love with him. The commissioner called him the face of the game after his performance in the Home Run Derby; the television ratings were the best in years and proof that baseball could indeed market its players.

All the game needed was someone as relatable as Judge—a good guy, polite, refreshingly devoid of bling. Even during the slump he'd still acted immensely likeable. There was no trace of frustration or anger on Judge's face or in his conversations with the press. He treated each day as it came and brushed aside questions about whether the strikeout streak or his current funk was weighing on him. But he did allow that he was disappointed about letting his teammates down.

"I want to be that guy in position with runners on every single time," he said. "It's a little disappointing not being able to get the job done, but there's nothing you can do about it. You can't pout. You can't cry. You've just got to keep working and move on."

The emergence of Aaron Judge catapulted the Yankees, which solidified the first AL wild card, into the postseason in 2017. He finished the regular season with a .284 batting average and led the American League in home runs (52), runs scored (128), walks (127), and strikeouts (208), and was second in runs batted in (114) and slugging percentage (.627). He put together one of the most memorable rookie seasons in history, setting records for most home runs and most walks by a first-year player. His numbers were staggering, but history says it's improbable to sustain such a torrid pace over a long career. Even if his stats return to the realm of a mere mortal superstar, his entertainment value and marketability is sure to remain through the roof. No matter how the rookie star continues to develop, all eyes are on Aaron Judge. It has been that way since he was a boy on the playgrounds of Linden.

TIMELINE

1992	• Born on April 26 in Linden, California, and was adopted a day later.
2006–2010	• Attended Linden High School, where he played baseball, football, and basketball.
2010	• Selected in the 31st round of the Major League Baseball Amateur Draft by the Oakland Athletics but elects to attend Fresno State University.
2011	• Named a Louisville Slugger Freshman All-American.
2012	• Won College Home Run Derby in Omaha.
2013	• Named All-Conference for the third consecutive season. • Selected in the first round (32nd overall) in the Major League Baseball Amateur Draft by the New York Yankees.
2014	• In his first professional season, hit a combined .308/.419/.486 with 17 HR and 78 RBIs in A-ball for Charleston and Tampa.
2015	• Invited to major-league spring training as a non-roster player. • Went 1-for-4 for the US team in the All-Star Futures Game in Cincinnati. • Hit 12 home runs in 63 games for Double-A Trenton before being promoted to Triple-A Scranton/Wilkes-Barre. • Hit combined .255/.330/.448 in 124 games.

2016	• Promoted to the major leagues on August 13 after hitting 19 home runs in 93 games for Scranton/ Wilkes-Barre and homered in his first major-league at-bat against Tampa Bay. • Became the second Yankees player in history to hit a home run in each of his first two major-league games.
2017	• Tied a major-league rookie record with 10 home runs in April and was named the American League Rookie of the Month. • Hit first career grand slam on May 28 against Oakland. • Named AL Rookie of the Month for May. • Named AL Player of the Week on June 12 after going 12-for-24 with three home runs, six RBIs, six walks, and 10 runs scored. • Set new Yankees team record for home runs by a rookie with his 30th on July 7 against Milwaukee, breaking Joe DiMaggio's mark set in 1936. • Leading vote-getter among AL players for the MLB All-Star Game. • Won 2017 Home Run Derby at Miami, beating Minnesota's Miguel Sanó in the finals. • Struck out in 37 consecutive games between July 8 and August 20, a major-league record. • Hit his 50th home run of the season on September 25 against the Royals, a single-season record for a rookie. • Hit his 52nd home run on September 30, surpassing Babe Ruth for the single-season record for most home runs by a Yankee at home.

BIBLIOGRAPHY

Articles

Apstein, Stephanie. "All Rise." *Sports Illustrated*, May 15, 2017.

Associated Press. "6-Foot-7 Aaron Judge Transforms Batting Practice in the Bronx." May 1, 2017.

Boland, Erik. "Aaron Judge Considers Himself an 'Underdog' to Win Yankees' Rightfield Job." *Newsday*, February 13, 2017.

Borzi, Pat. "Aaron Judge Shrugs Off Slump, Then Delivers Two Hits in Yankees' Win." *New York Times*, July 18, 2017.

Clair, Michael, and Bryan Hoch. "Aaron Judge Now Has Very Own Judge's Chambers Section at Yankee Stadium." MLB.com, May 23, 2017.

Curran, Aidan. "Aaron Judge 'Can Become the Face of the Game,' Says MLB Commissioner Rob Manfred." YESNetwork.com, July 11, 2017.

ESPN.com. "Bryce Harper, Aaron Judge Top Fan Vote." July 2, 2017.

Feinsand, Mark. "Yankees Prospect Aaron Judge Has a Huge Future in Pinstripes." *New York Daily News*, March 7, 2015.

Gligich, Daniel. "Aaron Judge, from Fresno to the Bronx." *Collegian*, September 13, 2016.

Grabar, Henry. "Aaron Judge Could Be the Face of Baseball." *Slate*, July 25, 2017.

Harper, John. "How Aaron Judge Became A Bomber: The Inside Story of the Yankees' Draft Strategy in 2013." *New York Daily News*, April 22, 2017.

Hickey, John. "The One Who Got Away Pays a Visit on the A's This Weekend." *Mercury News*, June 15, 2017.

Iseman, Chris. "Aaron Judge's Chipped Tooth Is Fixed, and He's in Yankees Lineup." *USA Today*, July 28, 2017.

Kernan, Kevin. "'Blessed' Yankees Prospect Elicits Stargell, Stanton Comps." *New York Post*, March 11, 2015.

Klocke, Mike. "Aaron Judge: From Linden's Cherry Country to the Big Apple." Recordnet.com, February 11, 2017.

Marchand, Andrew. "Inside Dirt: Aaron Judge Has a Special Plan to Break His Slump." ESPN.com, July 18, 2017.

Martinelli, Michelle. "Aaron Judge Reminds Himself Every Day How Bad He Was Last Year." *USA Today*, July 8, 2017.

Mazzeo, Mike. "Aaron Judge's Latest Home Run Proves He Is the Most Exciting Baby Bomber." *New York Daily News*, April 20, 2017.

———. "Aaron Judge's Yankees Teammates React to His Moonshot at Safeco Field." *New York Daily News*, July 22, 2017.

Miller, Andrew. "Future Yankees Star? He'll Be Judge of That." *Post and Courier*, April 5, 2014.

Mooney, Roger. "Yankees RF Aaron Judge Hurts Rays with Glove, Not Bat." *Tampa Bay Times*, May 21, 2017.

Petit, Stephanie. "Home Run Derby Winner Aaron Judge's Amazing Journey from Adoption to MLB All-Star." *People*, July 11, 2017.

Rieber, Anthony. "Yankees Manager Joe Girardi Sees Some Derek Jeter in Aaron Judge." *Newsday*, May 2, 2017.

Santasiere, Alfred. "Judge-ment Day." *Yankees Magazine*, March 2016.

Serby, Steve. "Aaron Judge Talks A-Rod, Yankees Spotlight and Mammoth HRs." *New York Post*, August 14, 2016.

Shaikin, Bill. "Yankees' Aaron Judge Puts on a Show in Home Run Derby." *Los Angeles Times*, July 10, 2017.

Sheinin, Dave. "Yankees Phenom Aaron Judge Is Tight End-Size, but Was Always a Baseball Player at Heart." *Washington Post*, May 31, 2017.

Suss, Nick. "Prospects Austin, Judge Go Deep in Debuts at Yankee Stadium." MLB.com, August 13, 2016.

Warszawski, Marek. "10 Facts to Impress Your Buddies with the Next Time Aaron Judges Smashes One." *Fresno Bee*, June 13, 2017.

Witz, Billy. "Aaron Judge Has the Power to Teach a Pitcher." *New York Times*, July 22, 2017.

Websites

Major League Baseball Statistics and History.
www.baseball-reference.com

Minor League Baseball Statistics and History.
www.thebaseballcube.com

National Baseball Hall of Fame and Museum.
www.baseballhalloffame.org

Official site of Aaron Judge.
www.mlb.com

Official site of the New York Yankees.
www.yankees.com

ABOUT THE AUTHOR

David Fischer has written for the *New York Times* and *Sports Illustrated for Kids* and has worked at *Sports Illustrated, National Sports Daily,* and NBC Sports. He is the author of several sports titles, including *Derek Jeter #2: Thanks for the Memories* and *Miracle Moments in New York Yankees History.* Fischer is also the editor of *Facing Mariano Rivera.* He resides in New Jersey.

To receive David Fischer's coverage of Aaron Judge's 2017 postseason, email info@skyhorsepublishing.com and ask for the epilogue to *Aaron Judge: The Incredible Story of the New York Yankees' Home Run–Hitting Phenom.*